LOST
CITIES
OF THE
ANCIENT
WORLD

Philip Matyszak

LOST
CITIES
OF THE
ANCIENT
WORLD

CONTENTS

Previous pages View over the amphitheatre in the Roman city of Timgad, in modern-day Algeria, which was founded by the emperor Trajan c. AD 100.

Left Inscription found at Dura-Europos invoking good fortune for the emperor, the senate and people of Rome.

Following pages The Sphinx Gate at the Hittite capital of Hattusa in modern-day Turkey. The city was founded in the Late Bronze Age, sixth millennium BC.

INTRODUCTION
Ghosts of the Past

Human development and the evolution of the city – in its manifold forms – are inextricably linked. In fact, one definition of modern humans is that we are a city-building species. Throughout history, people have been drawn to cities because that is where the action is – where almost all human progress has taken place. We tend to think of cities as huge metropolises, home to tens of thousands of people, yet even today that is not always the case. In North America, 'cities' with populations of fewer than five thousand people are not uncommon. In the ancient world a 'city' could be even smaller, and how these mini-cities functioned tells us much about early societies.

Archaeologists piecing together our human story once believed that urbanization represented the natural next step after the invention of agriculture. The logic went that farming peoples had a newfound sense of investment in the land, which they needed to defend against the most violent and predatory species on the planet – other humans. Where natural defences did not exist in the local geography, people built them, and these defensive strongholds were the first cities.

Yet it now appears that such a view reflects an unnecessarily gloomy opinion of humanity. Modern research has shown that even non-agricultural peoples were fond of each other's company, and congregated in large numbers for reasons that had nothing to do with warfare. Consider Göbekli Tepe in Anatolia, where archaeologists have found massive stone structures comparable to Stonehenge, but better carved and six thousand years older.

The construction required a coordinated effort over thousands of hours by pre-agricultural peoples. Other evidence, for example at Dolní Věstonice in the Czech Republic, shows that 'nomadic' humans periodically gathered in large numbers, for reasons about which we can only speculate. These settlements, for all that they were temporary, were the size of many of the ancient cities described in this book.

Also, the first cities did not appear on highly defensible mountaintops but on flat agricultural plains, such as those along the Nile in Egypt, the Euphrates in Mesopotamia and the Yellow River in China. Rivers provide not only fresh water, but also opportunities for travel and trade. Cities apparently, therefore, developed not primarily for military reasons but to leverage agricultural surplus by gathering a non-farming population for the purposes of government, religion, education and trade. The first cities were a collective human effort, of which war was but one aspect.

Cities were constructed for a variety of reasons. Persepolis, 'The City of the Persians', was largely a ceremonial site and was almost deserted at certain times of the year, yet was of huge significance to the empire. Some cities, such as Roman Waldgirmes in Germany, were founded as explicit statements of empire, while others, such as Mardaman in Mesopotamia, grew from trading stations and caravan stops. Or a city might exist as a purely administrative and religious centre, in which the actual population lived outside the city walls, doing what almost everyone in the pre-modern world did: farming for a living.

Indeed, where ancient people did live in a city, most did the opposite of the modern commute – they left the city in the morning to work in the fields outside – and the size of the population was irrelevant to a city's status. What mattered was that the city was a self-governing entity that provided administrative and policing services to the surrounding countryside, and it is this definition that we apply to the ancient cities in this book. Even a tiny settlement, such as Skara Brae in the Orkney Islands, would count as a 'city' to the locals if there was nothing of comparable size for hundreds of kilometres around. Urbanism is relative.

Over the centuries the world changed, as did our ways of living, and some cities were no longer needed, wanted or fit for purpose. Today the remains of the city of Uruk, the largest settlement in Mesopotamia in the fourth millennium BC, sit forlornly in a barren landscape, abandoned after desertification claimed the once-fertile surrounding fields. Also in Mesopotamia is proud Akkad, once a thriving city. Then its king fell out with the gods, and its people believed that his city was thereafter destroyed by divine vengeance – and indeed destroyed so comprehensively that its location is now unknown.

Other cities have been abandoned for more prosaic reasons. A once-thriving port silted up, trade routes shifted, better crops could be grown in a more distant valley. After the fall of the Roman empire in the west, some cities were left with everything but inhabitants. Places like Venta Silurum in modern Wales were not abandoned

because they were unliveable, but because there was no reason to live there any more. Timgad and Hattusa were great metropolises of their day, but now exist mostly as passing references in textbooks. Places such as this we count as lost cities.

Once a city is lost, it may live on in myth – think of Troy, Camelot and Atlantis – or it might vanish completely from the collective consciousness of humankind, until its footprint is found. Doubtless there exist, beneath the sea, soil or desert sands, hundreds of such cities, lost and forgotten so completely that they have entirely dropped out of the human story – for now, at least.

Many of the abandoned cities in this book are places we can visit, wander the empty streets and imagine what life was like there, all those centuries ago. Sometimes the wandering must be done with an aqualung, and sometimes the political convulsions of the modern world make tourism unrealistically hazardous. Occasionally the actual location has been forgotten. But the cities are still there, nevertheless, timeless, silent reminders of other times, other places and very different ways of life. For all their past glories, they are inhabited now only by ghosts of the past, and so count as 'lost'.

To count as 'forgotten', a city must have at some point dropped off the map, its former significance so obliterated that even the presence of the city's ruins are barely remembered. Such a one is Cyrene in Libya, once a vibrant trading centre and one of the major cities of the southern Mediterranean. Yet changing times and creeping desertification have left only a beautiful location and ruins that no-one visited for centuries.

Some of the cities described here – such as Troy – are not at all forgotten (though Troy was, for a while, so profoundly lost that people believed it to be only a myth). Yet these cities remain only as relics of a lost culture, casualties of changing times and circumstance that have also left lost Roman cities in Algeria and Greek cities in Egypt. Other cities, such as Dura-Europos and Beta Samati, are closer to being genuinely forgotten, yet they also have rich histories well worth exploring.

These are cities that were thriving communities in their prime, but which were destroyed – sometimes by a changing climate, sometimes as deliberate acts of devastation, but also simply through changing circumstances that removed the reason for their existence. Whether in a desert setting, beside (or under) the sea, or incongruous in a modern landscape, all such cities have their own unique stories – stories which remind us that for millennia, despite the barbarism, crimes and follies of mankind, people have always rather liked living together. These different peoples and cultures fought and traded between themselves, exchanging inventions, ideas and philosophies along the way, with the result that peoples as far apart as Sudan in Africa and the Orkney Islands in Scotland shared much of a common heritage.

Their cities, lost and forgotten as they may be, are that heritage written in stone.

A funerary panel from Palmyra shows the deceased waking in the afterlife to a bowl of wine brought by an attendant. The fusion of cultures in this cosmopolitan city is shown by the Parthian clothing of the subjects and the Greco-Roman style of the relief.

PART ONE
The Oldest Cities

Which came first: the chicken or the egg? Or, to look at the question through the eyes of archaeologists and anthropologists studying the first human cities, which came first: the city or the farm?

Even a few decades ago this question would have seemed nonsensical. Conventional wisdom stated that, as humans learned the joys of agriculture, they settled down, abandoned their hunter-gatherer lifestyles and began to produce enough food to support a non-farming population of priests, administrators and merchants. This non-farming population worked most efficiently with a large number of people living in close proximity, and so the city was born.

However, some unsettling evidence from the first cities seems to challenge this view. We now know that our climate is far from constant. We are currently living in an Ice Age, although in a period of inter-glacial warming that began around twenty thousand years ago. In fact, the early Neolithic era of some ten thousand years ago seems to have been warmer and wetter than conditions today. In some parts of the world, especially in the area between Anatolia and the Iranian plateau, conditions were particularly benign. Wetlands supported substantial stocks of wildfowl and fish, and extensive meadows, rich in natural grains, were grazed by herds of wild goats and deer. It seems that the land may have been rich enough to support a settled population of hunter-gatherers, so the hunter-gatherers on that land promptly settled down.

The first cities seem to have been tribal encampments on a larger scale. Significantly, what is missing are signs of administrators, priests and merchants. Çatalhöyük, for example, had no temples, large marketplaces or palaces.

Much of ancient northern America was, at times, a huge freshwater lake, and some eight thousand years ago this abruptly released millions of tonnes of glacial meltwater. The new hypothesis is that this led to a sharp drop in global temperatures and the subsequent drying up of once-fertile wetlands. Humans living in urban settlements were reluctant to leave homes established for generations, and so used their ingenuity to make the most of what remained. Dry meadows were fertilized and irrigated, and wild grains domesticated. Also domesticated were the animals which grazed upon those grains.

In short, humans may not have developed cities as a result of surplus from agriculture. Instead, humans already living in cities might have turned to agriculture so that they could keep on living in their cities. Agriculture, especially if based upon irrigation, does require a degree of organization and administration to co-ordinate the distribution of surplus and to sort out disputes, which the first kings did in their newly built palaces. A new dependence on the weather required the placating of gods, who needed temples. Cities began to share resources through trade, and so a merchant class was born.

Many of the cities of this era were not able to cope with changing times and were abandoned. Others vanished beneath the

waters of shifting coastlines. Competition
for resources brought about a new human
invention – organized warfare – and
some cities were either indefensible or
no longer worth defending. Yet this did
not happen overnight. The evolution of
human development from the Neolithic to
the Bronze Age was a slow, patchy process.
Some cities that became redundant, and
were abandoned, did so after enduring
for centuries longer than well-established
cities of the modern era such as Berlin,
Moscow and Paris.

One thing that did not alter in a changing
world was the growth of urbanism. Having
decided that they liked living in cities,
humans continued to do so. The first cities
are the physical embodiment of human
resilience in the face of (sometimes self-
inflicted) adversity. Whether on isolated
northern islands, fighting off encroaching
desert sands or rising seas, or expanding
onto the lands of indignant pastoralists, the
humans of the first cities battled the odds
– and each other – to lay the foundations
of the world that we know today.

c. 7250–5500 BC
Çatalhöyük
Expectations

City travel was a matter of picking a location and direction and then walking across rooftops until one arrived.

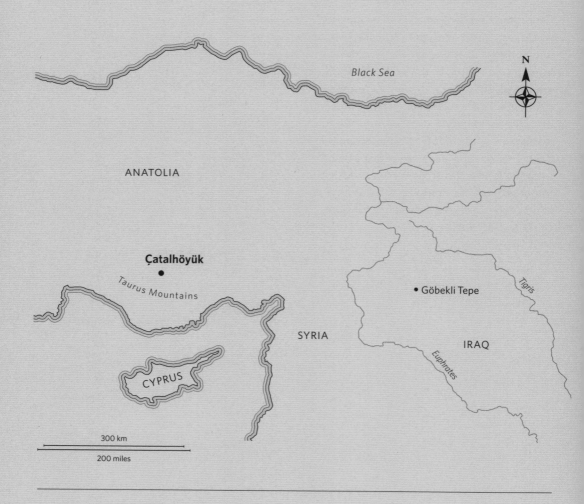

In the twentieth century, most anthropologists had a reasonably clear idea about how modern society had developed. Humans in Mesopotamia developed agriculture, and the surplus from farming allowed them to live in larger, denser units and support non-farmers, such as priests and soldiers. Because large communities need to be organized, townspeople developed hierarchies which ran from king to peasant, with the soldiers keeping order. While the early pre-urban societies had been matriarchal and largely worshipped earth deities, these new societies were fiercely patriarchal and worshipped sky gods. Gradually the agricultural and urban revolution spread around the world to create modern civilization as we know it.

Now, a rediscovered city is challenging these assumptions. In fact, the city has been described by UNESCO as 'a key site for understanding human prehistory' – a claim which might be considered hyperbole, were it not for the fact that the discoveries there are radically changing how human prehistory is viewed.

For a start, the city of Çatalhöyük is not in Mesopotamia but in central Anatolia, almost 1,500 kilometres (930 miles) to

Interior of a house in Çatalhöyük, with one area screened off by the 'bull's horn' motif that was a common feature of houses in the city.

The densely packed houses of Çatalhöyük in a modern landscape, which would have appeared unimaginably arid to the city's original inhabitants.

the northwest. And while Uruk in Mesopotamia had long been considered the world's oldest city, Çatalhöyük is at least as early, with a foundation date around nine thousand years ago, and possibly before. The people of this extremely ancient settlement were basically inventing the concept of large-scale communal living as they went along.

Consequently, Çatalhöyük has some surprising aspects. For example, there were no graveyards, but instead people were buried beneath platforms in their homes. Houses were often infilled, burned and rebuilt, creating eighteen layers of housing before the city was abandoned before 5500 BC (a mere 4,700 years or so before the foundation of Rome). Also, Çatalhöyük did not have streets. Instead, the houses were built right beside each other. The occupants came and went through the same openings in the flat roofs that allowed smoke to exit from their windowless rooms.

This concept of urban planning allowed for considerable housing density, with over two thousand houses packed into the 12-hectare (30-acre) site. City travel was a matter of picking a location and direction and then walking across rooftops until one arrived. The only interruption came where a small river flowed between the hillocks which made up the site, dividing a larger, older mound on the east side from a smaller, newer one to the west.

This division gives the city its name (meaning 'Forked Tumulus' in modern Turkish), because a footpath that ran through the area before it was excavated forked at this point. It is not known what the inhabitants of Çatalhöyük called their city, or even if it had a name. Names are needed to distinguish a thing from similar things, and there was nothing like Çatalhöyük in the locality, or indeed perhaps anywhere in the world.

Also, while agriculture was known to the population and grew in importance as time went on, at the time of its foundation Çatalhöyük seems to have been inhabited mainly by hunter-gatherers. The area is now one of the driest parts of Turkey, but nine thousand years ago it was a fertile wetland and rich enough in wildlife and plants to support a static population. Fish, water birds, wild sheep and cattle provided protein, while wheat, barley, pistachios and almonds were among the plants that were harvested locally. Consequently, rather than agriculture leading to urbanism, as has always been believed, Çatalhöyük's urbanism may have led to agriculture, as the city developed farming to support a population that eventually grew to around eight thousand inhabitants.

This alone might have been sufficient to make Çatalhöyük a truly remarkable city, but the surprises have kept coming. Almost all the site is taken up by housing. No public spaces have yet been discovered – no palaces, basilicas, markets, temples or theatres. (By way of comparison, almost two-thirds of central Rome in antiquity was taken up by public space of one type or another.) Particularly notable is the lack of any palace or temple.

If Çatalhöyük had a centralized administration, there are no signs of it. The place seems remarkably egalitarian, for all the houses so far excavated share a similar layout, and none is more particularly ornate than the others. It seems that decisions were taken collectively. Similarly, some property in the city appears to have been used by whoever needed it at the time. Some anthropologists have argued that this means that the city was fiercely egalitarian. Perhaps the residents simply did not know how to be otherwise, since autocracy as an administrative system may not yet have been invented.

The first digs by archaeologists revealed a large number of female figurines, which led to the assumption that Çatalhöyük was a matriarchal society. This concept has been enthusiastically adopted by some, but again Çatalhöyük has resisted stereotypes. Further excavations have turned up large numbers of male figurines and animals. Once again, Çatalhöyük seems to have been egalitarian – examination of skeletons shows that men and women had similar diets and were buried with the same honours. Furthermore, soot from indoor fires, which entered the lungs and ended up as deposits on skeletal ribs, shows that men and women spent an equal amount of time indoors. Wear on bones suggests that male and female workers performed much the same tasks, though paintings indicate that men did most of the big-game hunting.

Ian Hodder, one of the archaeologists who excavated the site, has commented, 'We are not witnessing a patriarchy or a matriarchy. What we are seeing is perhaps more interesting – a society in which, in many areas, the question of whether you were a man or a woman did not determine the life you could lead.' One difference, naturally, is that it was the women who gave birth – with all the risks that childbirth entailed in the pre-modern era. It has been noted that women with neonatal children were buried nearest the hearth in most houses.

There is much about Çatalhöyük that remains to be discovered. Yet the picture which has emerged so far is appealing. There is little evidence that the weapons discovered there were used for anything other than hunting, so Çatalhöyük may have been a peaceful society. It has been argued that ancient peoples did not build their homes on high ground just for the view (after multiple rebuildings, Çatalhöyük stood some 20 metres [65 feet] above the surrounding plain), but in this case avoiding flooding might have been a more serious consideration than defence.

The weapons were made of horn and chipped obsidian, and imported artefacts showed that the people of the city had trade links with locations in Syria. The houses were of plastered mud-brick and lavishly decorated with paintings and sculptures. Actual and carved skulls of wild animals feature strongly – with bulls, deer, leopards and vultures among the creatures so depicted. There are even tantalizing hints that some of the world's first metalworkers mined and smelted the local lead deposits.

Çatalhöyük was eventually abandoned. The drying of the area may have made it less productive, and possibly the development of new ideas about urban environments, such as the need for streets and public spaces, eventually made Çatalhöyük less appealing. In later years, objects such as stamp seals show that concepts such as private property were gaining traction, and certainly farming was by then a major industry (the first cattle were domesticated at about this time). The abandonment of the city has left remarkably well-preserved remains, where doubtless further surprises await to make us rethink yet more of our ideas about humanity's ancient past.

Limestone 'earth-mother' figurines were among the first found at the site and led some early researchers to believe that Çatalhöyük had a matriarchal society.

Çatalhöyük Today

After being abandoned, the ruins of Çatalhöyük were gradually buried by time and spent the next six thousand years as a pair of unassuming hillocks on Turkey's Konya plain. The first archaeologist to take an interest was an Englishman called James Mellaart, who found the site in 1958 and excavated it in 1961–65. It was Mellaart's discovery of female figurines that led to the belief in a matriarchal society, which later investigations towards the end of the twentieth century have largely overturned.

There is now an international community of experts at Çatalhöyük who work together in an interdisciplinary team called the Çatalhöyük Research Project, dedicated to unravelling the mysteries of human prehistory at the site. Since 2012, Çatalhöyük has been a UNESCO World Heritage Site and the Turkish Directorate General of Monuments and Museums carefully limits the visits of outsiders, including tourists.

There is a small visitor reception centre at Çatalhöyük, and a café and a museum containing replica artefacts, but no-one is allowed to wander around unescorted. Much of the excavated portion of the site is now covered by large shelters which protect the excavated ruins from the elements.

c. 3200–2500 BC
Skara Brae
Living Rough in the Orkneys

Because there were no trees, the islanders built their homes from stone, including the furniture.

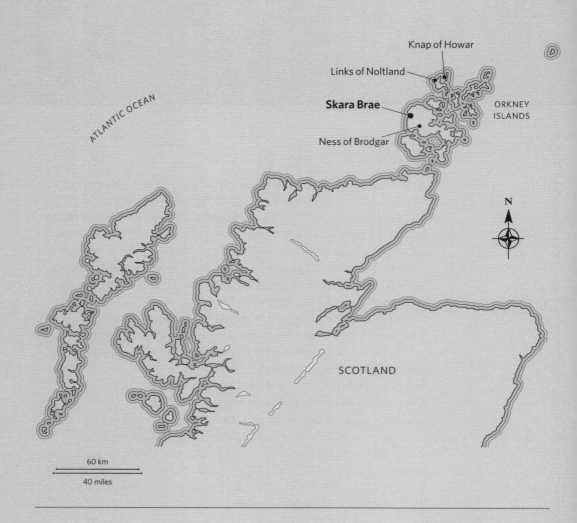

Knap of Howar

Links of Noltland

Skara Brae

ORKNEY ISLANDS

Ness of Brodgar

ATLANTIC OCEAN

N

SCOTLAND

60 km

40 miles

The conventional theory of human civilization (with farming surplus leading to ever-larger settlements) has taken a few dents recently. Some early settlements actually pre-date widespread agriculture, and some were established in territory far from ideal for cultivation. Such was Skara Brae, a settlement in the windswept Orkney Islands, north of the Scottish mainland, where people seem to have decided on collective living over five thousand years ago despite the lack of fertile fields, abundant wildlife, and fruit trees – or indeed trees of any kind.

We do not know why people first chose to live at Skara Brae, nor the extent of the original settlement, because much of it may have been lost to the sea before anyone in the modern era even realized it had been there. Other houses on the site may have been cruder constructions that are now completely eroded away. Indeed, without these powerful erosive forces Skara Brae might never have been discovered at all.

Interior of a home at Skara Brae, where you could have any type of furniture you liked – as long as it was stone.

In the winter of 1850 a powerful storm hit Scotland, causing numerous deaths. On the largest of the Orkney Islands – which the inhabitants call Mainland – the winds were channelled with particular ferocity by the shape of the Bay of Skaill to focus upon a particular knoll known to locals as the Mound by the Reef, or 'Skerrabra'. The winds stripped away the loose sandy earth to reveal a cluster of roofless houses grouped together and linked by covered passageways.

The local laird, William Watt, immediately began some amateur archaeological excavations, and contacted Orcadian antiquarian George Petrie to investigate the site. At first, Skara Brae was believed to be an Iron Age settlement and therefore some 3,500 years younger and less interesting than it really is. Today, thanks to radiocarbon dating and further excavations, Skara Brae is recognized as perhaps the best-preserved Neolithic site in Europe.

Around 3200 BC, when Skara Brae was first settled, the landscape was somewhat different. The rolling fields were still there, and the pristine sandy beaches – but the coastline has changed over the centuries. The Skara Brae settlement was originally much further inland, probably built near where a freshwater lagoon was once separated from the ocean by sand dunes.

Because there were no trees, the islanders built their homes from stone, including the furniture. In the houses discovered so

Whalebone carvings from Skara Brae. Crude though they are, these are among the vanishingly few surviving representations of humans from Britain's Neolithic era.

far, these furnishings seem to have been remarkably consistent. The basic building material was flagstones derived from naturally occurring sedimentary rock. The builders seem to have dug slightly into the side of the knoll to give earth support to the walls, and then stacked the flagstones one atop the other without the benefit of mortar. There is no sign of any roofs, which means these must have been made of organic material which rotted away millennia ago.

One possibility for the roofs would be mats of seaweed weighed down by straw ropes attached to stones. This is certainly practical and was the technique used by inhabitants of the Orkney archipelago until relatively recently. Whalebone or driftwood might have supplied the roof beams, but one might expect to find evidence of such relatively durable materials if these were indeed used.

A distinctive feature of the cluster of houses discovered so far is that a small antechamber connected each house to a drain, by which storm water flushed effluent to the sea. It is reasonable to suppose that the antechambers were toilets, and that this was one of the world's earliest sewer systems. Given the bitter cold and howling storms of an Orkney winter, there would be a strong incentive to answer calls of nature without exposing oneself to the elements, and indoor privies would allow just that.

Skara Brae's stone furnishings have survived, where the wooden furniture of much later British settlements has not. In each house

Previous pages 'City' is a relative term. Though barely qualifying as a hamlet today, Skara Brae was by far the largest settlement in the region and probably known to its inhabitants simply as 'the city'.

there was a bed on either side of the main entrance. It is probable that the husband slept on the larger one and the wife on the smaller, with young offspring sharing the beds with their parents, as was common until the early modern era. In the centre of a Skara Brae home was the stone-built hearth. Storage cupboards still stand in the corners of the square rooms, with chairs beside them and dressers which once held pottery.

In fact, remnants of that pottery have helped to date Skara Brae. The fragments found are of a type called Grooved Ware, and the presence of these pots shows that even at this early date the Orkneys were connected by trade routes to the rest of Britain. There is a fascinating possibility that this style of pot – now found at Neolithic sites across Britain – actually originated in the Orkneys and spread from there to Britain and Ireland.

One mysterious discovery at Skara Brae has been of stone balls, painstakingly carved with indecipherable lines and patterns. Nobody knows their purpose, though early archaeologists came up with fanciful accounts of island mystics practising their secret rites away from the mainland.

In fact, it seems that Skara Brae was mainly a colony of sheep farmers. One could get a lot of mileage out of a sheep in the Neolithic era. The ram's horns provided drinking vessels, tools and musical instruments. The bones provided glue and needles, while the sinews were used as thread. These materials could be used to stitch leather made from sheepskin, while the wool could be woven, or pounded with the glue to make felt. The bladder made a handy container, and the intestines held ground meat in a sausage. While alive, ewes provided milk, and dead they became steaks roasted over a fire fuelled by dried sheep's dung.

It appears that at least one of the houses in the cluster discovered so far was a sort of manufactory where tools, including perhaps leatherwork items, were made for trade and use. No weapons have been found, unless one counts bone knives and crude axes, but these were more probably tools – nothing about the location of the houses suggests a need to defend against anything but the weather.

Six or seven hundred years after people started living there, Skara Brae was abandoned. Beads from a broken necklace strewn across the floor of one of the houses were once taken as evidence of an urgent evacuation in the face of an environmental threat. However, this threat could not have been too violent as no human remains have yet been found. The houses themselves were becoming steadily encased by the mounting debris of rubbish from the settlement and covered by sand from drifting dunes, so it seems

Carved between four and five thousand years ago, these mysterious stones have fascinated and bewildered archaeologists of the modern era.

likely that the inhabitants gradually departed for more hospitable places. Skara Brae was left to sink beneath the sands that would cover it for the next forty centuries.

Skara Brae Today

Intrepid travellers to the Orkneys can visit Skara Brae between April and September after paying a small fee to the Historic Scotland organization, which has the site in its care.

The site does need care, for the seawall built to protect the buildings a century ago is struggling against rising tides and increasingly ferocious weather. There is a risk that a storm of the intensity that originally revealed Skara Brae to modern eyes might finish the job and destroy it altogether.

Since 1999 Skara Brae has been a UNESCO World Heritage Site. Archaeological research has continued, with the hope that more buildings will be discovered and the full extent of the settlement finally revealed.

c. 3200–2000 BC
Akkad
The Cursed City

The old women wailed 'Alas for my city!'
and the old men echoed 'Alas for its people!'

Curse of Agade, line 198

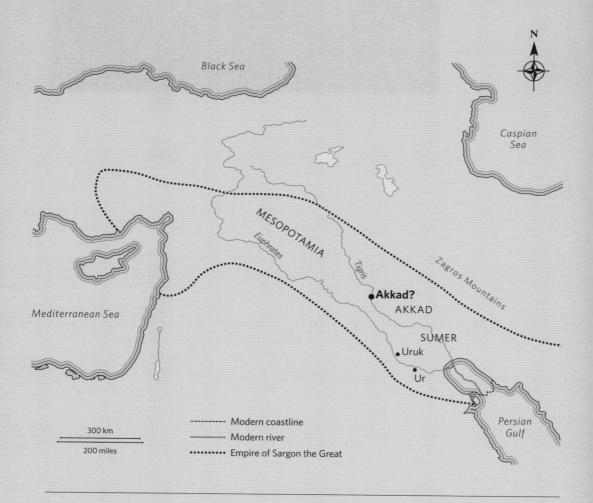

Black Sea

Caspian
Sea

MESOPOTAMIA

Euphrates

Tigris

Zagros Mountains

●**Akkad?**

AKKAD

SUMER

●Uruk

●Ur

Mediterranean Sea

Persian
Gulf

N

300 km

200 miles

---------- Modern coastline
················ Modern river
●●●●●● Empire of Sargon the Great

For reasons which are still fiercely debated, humans began large-scale city construction around 4500 BC. This endeavour took off first in the area today encompassed by southern Iraq, western Iran and eastern Syria, along an arc known as 'The Fertile Crescent'. The ancient city of Uruk was perhaps the first of these settlements, but it was quickly followed by others that sprang up on the banks of the Tigris and Euphrates rivers. Modern convention follows the ancient Greeks in calling this area Mesopotamia, which simply means 'between rivers'.

One such early city was Agade, later known as Akkad. It was founded at a river crossing: possibly on the Tigris near modern Baghdad, or alternatively on the western bank of the Euphrates near the Sumerian city of Mari. The latter location may be likelier, because most of the information that we have about Akkad comes from cuneiform texts on clay tablets excavated from Mari.

Before the Mari cuneiform tablets were deciphered in the nineteenth century, all that was known of Agade/Akkad was a single reference in the Bible. 'Nimrod ... was a mighty hunter ... And the beginning of his kingdom was Babel, and Erech, and Accad, and Calneh, in the land of Shinar' (Genesis 10.8–10).

Nothing is known of the early history of Agade, which might have passed unnoticed from the annals of history had not a child called Sargon been born there some time before 2300 BC. Sargon founded what is generally considered to be the world's first empire. In the decades before his rise to power, some Mesopotamian cities had formed close alliances, approximating to nations, but Sargon was

Akkadian cylinder seal (left) and the image after the seal has been rolled onto a clay surface (right). Bull-man versus lion was a common theme, though the underlying myth is unknown. The inscription tells us that this was the seal of one Ishri-ilum.

the first to build a true empire (defined as a multinational entity
ruled by a central power).

In a surviving inscription, Sargon claims to have founded Akkad,
which city gave its name to his dominion – the Akkadian empire.
However, Sargon's Akkad was quite certainly a rebranded version
of the already ancient city of Agade. (The name 'Agade' pre-dates
the Semitic language used by Sargon in his inscriptions.) Doubtless
Sargon did substantially rebuild his home town during his long reign
(2334–2279 BC), and Akkad was a flourishing capital city thereafter.

After Sargon, the greatest of the Akkadian kings was his grandson
Naram-Sin, who reigned 2254–2218 BC, though all dates from this era
are disputed. Records are scant and fragmentary – not least because
the time between Naram-Sin and Cleopatra of Egypt is greater
than the time between Cleopatra and the invention of the television.

The people of Akkad built a temple for Naram-Sin after he
crushed a rebellion. This fact came to light when a modern road-
building project in Iraq unearthed a statue that recorded the event.
Known as the Bassetki Statue after the village near which it was
discovered, this bears an inscription in Akkadian. Since Bassetki
is in modern Kurdistan, the statue demonstrates how the culture
of Akkad had spread to other parts of the empire. The Akkadians
also standardized weights and measures and instituted an empire-
wide dating system, naming each year after a major event.

A separate inscription informs us that Naram-Sin's temple
in Akkad shared the city with at least one other major religious
building, for Akkad was a centre of worship of 'holy Inana', the
Semitic goddess of love, sensuality and fertility – and also of war.
Inana's temple in Akkad was a sanctuary and is described as a
'women's domain'.

A description of Akkad, written over a hundred years after
the reign of Naram-Sin, tells of city walls 'like a mountainside'
and a harbour where ships rested at peace, and claims that, just
as the Tigris flowed into the sea, so did the people of Sumeria
bring goods to Akkad in their boats (*Curse of Agade* lines 40–42).
The chronicle goes on: 'Like a girl setting up her quarters in the
women's part of the house, holy Inana embellished her city.' She
ensured that the warehouses were filled, and that the people had all
they could desire of food and drink. The courtyards were filled with
exotic sights – not just visitors from strange places but monkeys,
water buffalo, thoroughbred dogs and shaggy-coated sheep which
stepped aside for mighty elephants, while lions, wild ibex and other
captured animals were displayed in cages. People thronged to the
entertainments, enjoyed dinner parties and the tigi drum resounded

in the streets. 'Tigi' was both an instrument and a type of music in ancient Babylon.

Elsewhere in the empire the lands were bathed in contentment, and the governors and temples of these lands wearied the customs officials at the Akkad city gates with the size and splendour of their offerings. In short, according to the ancient chronicle summarized above, Akkad enjoyed a golden age.

This idyllic period ended when, for some unknown reason, the great god Enlil became displeased with Akkad. Even Inana could not stand against Enlil and she fled from the city. According to the tale, Naram-Sin waited, prayed and sacrificed to Enlil to find the reason for the god's displeasure, but seven years later he was still waiting. Finally, the exasperated king marched on Ekur, Enlil's sacred mountain temple. There he set up ladders and tore down the god's house brick by brick.

This act of sacrilege turned the other gods against Naram-Sin and his city. The chronicle records that, as it had been in the time before cities existed, the wide fields yielded no grain, the wetlands were devoid of fish, the orchards no longer provided syrup or wine, the clouds did not bring rain and plants did not grow. The price of oil and grain skyrocketed and the poor lay starving on the roofs of their houses. Violence and bloodshed became everyday events, and so packed were the streets with feral dogs that people walking alone or in pairs were torn apart. The old women wailed 'Alas for my city!' and the old men echoed 'Alas for its people!' (*Curse of Agade* line 198).

Foreign invaders were quick to fall upon the struggling empire, and Akkad's last kings were left to defend a city-state shrunken to a few fields beyond the city walls, until even these were lost. 'And so it was. On the tow-paths beside the canals the grass grew long, on the highways made for wagons, the grass of mourning grew' (*Curse of Agade* lines 272–74).

Akkad Today

For years the tale of the cursed city was regarded as just that – a tale, not as vivid as the *Iliad* of Homer but just as fictional. Then it was discovered that Troy actually existed, and there was more than a grain of truth in Homer's epic. So it has been with the story of Akkad.

Modern research looks upon the *Curse of Agade* not as a morality tale about the folly of challenging the gods, but as an account of societal collapse caused by climate change. The crops may indeed have failed and the rivers dried up, but owing to a major drought

Clay 'prism' in cuneiform script. To the eternal gratitude of later historians, this four-sided tablet contains a detailed list of the kings of Sumeria, from legendary times to the contemporary, along with details of their reigns.

rather than the wrath of Enlil. Geological research has revealed layers of lifeless soil around contemporary Mesopotamian cities, and drilling has shown strata of undersea dust deposited by ancient windstorms blowing across arid plains.

Whether victim of a changing climate or the fury of a god, Akkad passed into memory and then into legend, and then was forgotten so completely that today no-one knows where the mighty walls and thronged courtyards of Sargon's imperial capital once stood.

c. 2800–c. 1100 BC
Pavlopetri
The Oldest Submerged City
in the Mediterranean

What we've got here is something which is two or even
three thousand years older than most of the submerged
cities which have been studied … it is uniquely complete.
Dr Nicholas Flemming, marine geo-archaeologist

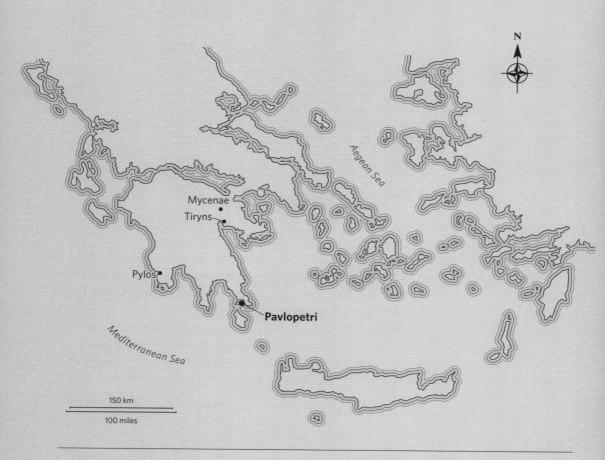

Three peninsulas stretch southward off the coast of Greece, making the Peloponnese look like the claws of a giant dragon reaching for Crete. Between the middle and eastern peninsulas lies the mouth of the River Eurotas, upstream of which are the remains of the ancient city of Sparta, founded around 950 BC. But Sparta is youthful compared to another city near the Laconian eastern peninsula, which was founded some two thousand years before.

What this city was called by its inhabitants is unknown. Today it is called Pavlopetri, after the tiny rocky islet that marks the outer edge of the underwater ruins. What we do know is that the inhabitants of ancient 'Pavlopetri' were cosmopolitan, expert builders and traders – especially in the fabrics that seem to have been a speciality in the area. At its peak around 1200 BC, the city was one of the many thriving ports of Mycenaean Greece. Pavlopetri stood beside a low-lying bay with long, sandy beaches and mountains all around.

Pavlopetri Island – an undistinguished rock outcrop that once stood above one of the oldest towns of prehistoric Greece.

The port was well situated for trade with Crete and, beyond that, Egypt. The rugged Laconian coastline offers few suitable harbours (the region was the terror of sailors in the ancient world) so Pavlopetri was able to flourish with scarcely any regional rivals. While the town survived the chaos which followed the end of the Mycenaean period in Greece, nothing could have saved it from the coming catastrophe. Rising sea levels, combined with several local earthquakes, produced a steady step-wise submergence of the ancient city, until storm waves finally broke into the built-up area and caused a total collapse. On the beach at Pounta the ruins still project from the sand, and continue under the sea.

The city beneath the waves. A diver hovers amid the digitally rendered remains of a domestic building in Vatika Bay. Much of the damage to the structures was caused by modern shipping.

The discovery of Pavlopetri

For modern archaeologists, the long-submerged slumber of Pavlopetri was an advantage. Few archaeological sites are completely pristine. Humans of later generations have the bad habit of wandering in and settling anew on sites, gradually burying them beneath their own buildings and debris. Because Pavlopetri has spent the last three

thousand years beneath the sea, the city remains frozen in time, a snapshot of how a late Mycenaean port city looked and functioned.

The centre was small and crowded. The core site is some 9,000 square metres (about 2 acres) in size (by comparison, London's Trafalgar Square is about 12,000 square metres). The surviving buildings consist of around fifteen densely packed complexes of structures of undressed stone, built back-to-back. A number of these were residential, as is shown by hearthstones and infant graves within the walls (a common funerary practice, gruesome as it seems to us). A larger communal cemetery lies just outside the city.

The overall settlement is larger, possibly 80,000 square metres (almost 20 acres), with scattered suburban houses of one or two storeys. The houses had large courtyards and small vegetable gardens; some were free-standing while others were what we would today call semi-detached. Pavlopetri was not randomly arranged but a tidily organized little city, with well-built roads and gutters to take away water brought in through carefully constructed channels. The flat-roofed buildings would have had roof gardens with fruit trees in pots, and washing hung out to dry safely beyond the reach of thieves.

Though there had been reports of a lost city in the area since 1904, it was not until 1967 that the city was rediscovered by marine geo-archaeologist Nicholas Flemming from the UK National Institute of Oceanography. After examining the submerged ridge that leads out to the islet of Pavlopetri and finding only drowned rock-cut tombs, he swam back across the small bay to the mainland and saw the sea floor covered in house foundations of uncut stones. He sketched these and arranged for a team of diving archaeologists from the University of Cambridge to survey the city in 1968. While the layout of the town was perfectly preserved, the buildings themselves were not. The sea above the settlement is only a few metres deep, and the dragging anchors of boats sheltering in Vatika Bay damaged many of the standing walls. In more recent years, large ships have used the waters off the island illegally to clean their hulls, and the caustic chemicals have damaged the already fragile site.

A cosmopolitan centre

Despite the degradation caused by marine activity and human interference, there remained much to excite the archaeologists who explored (and are still exploring) the ancient port. The team from Cambridge originally estimated that the city was founded in the Mycenaean era. That quickly changed when items were brought to the surface from the early Bronze Age, showing that Pavlopetri was settled much earlier, by 2800 BC at the latest. This makes Pavlopetri by some margin the oldest undersea city ever discovered. New finds at Pavlopetri, such as tools made of obsidian and Neolithic pottery, may yet push the age of that settlement back even further.

The shallow waters that caused the city to be discovered have also exposed the site to the effects of tidal and wave action, with underwater swells rolling and eventually breaking lighter artefacts, which would have survived at greater depths. One great advantage is that the ancient city is easily reached and explored with nothing more complicated than basic scuba gear. However, this is also a major disadvantage. Until recently the site was unpoliced, but once the location was known amateur souvenir hunters began to help themselves to artefacts that, left in context, would have told archaeologists a great deal more of the city's story. For example, it is known that the city's people were industrious weavers, because a common find is the circular stones used to hold in place the threads on a vertical loom. There are many more of these weights than have been discovered at other sites of the same antiquity, which suggests that cloth was produced for export. There are indications that the city had scribes, merchants and bronzeworkers as well as weavers. Doubtless there were also farmers and shepherds who worked outside the walls and kept the city supplied with basic foodstuffs.

Relics from the site show the city's cosmopolitan nature – even everyday items such as jugs and urns were either imported or show the influence of other civilizations around the Mediterranean, such as Egypt and Minoan Crete. Sadly, wave action has reduced most of these artefacts to sherds scattered across the seabed. Nevertheless, that Pavlopetri was a bustling port can be deduced from the number and nature of these sherds, many of which were from containers used to transport and store olive oil, exotic perfumes and dyes. From the concentration of sherds in specific areas, archaeologists have worked out that there were several large warehouses.

One of the most important places in a Mycenaean city was the megaron, a large hall-like room which served as the focus of administration and religious functions and as a place for merchants and traders to gather. One of the more exciting recent finds at Pavlopetri has been the discovery of a large structure which appears to have been an early version of one such megaron. This and other buildings that illustrate how the people of the city lived and worked have been brought to life by modern technological advances such as 3D sonar mapping, which has allowed the reconstruction of Pavlopetri's buildings in unprecedented detail. In fact, Pavlopetri was the first site to be mapped in this way.

Pavlopetri Today

The world that Pavlopetri left behind has not been kind to the archaeological remains, and until recently things were only getting worse. Alongside the continued theft of artefacts from the site, new infrastructure developments in the region, such as a natural gas pipeline and nearby power plant, have affected the waters in the bay. Fortunately, due to the work of local activists, the Greek authorities have now responded to the issue.

Since 2016 Pavlopetri has been a World Monuments Fund Watch site, which has led the Greek Ministry of Culture to take further steps to protect the site and encourage responsible visits. The Ephorate of Underwater Antiquities now offers guided tours of Pavlopetri. The Hydrographic Service of the Greek Navy now lists the location of the site on marine charts to ensure that the masters of larger vessels are aware of the risks that their crafts pose to Pavlopetri , and buoys have been set up to mark the boundaries of the site in an effort to prevent small boats from inadvertently damaging the ruins.

Prehistoric burials at Pavlopetri have been found underwater, dug into rock along the coast and in the dunes of the beach, as shown here.

It is ironic that ships, once the lifeblood of the ancient port, are now being steered away from Pavlopetri to ensure the survival of the city's remains.

Zoar
The City That Lived

Lot pleaded that he might be allowed to shelter in the nearby city of Zoar, and the angel agreed to spare the town.

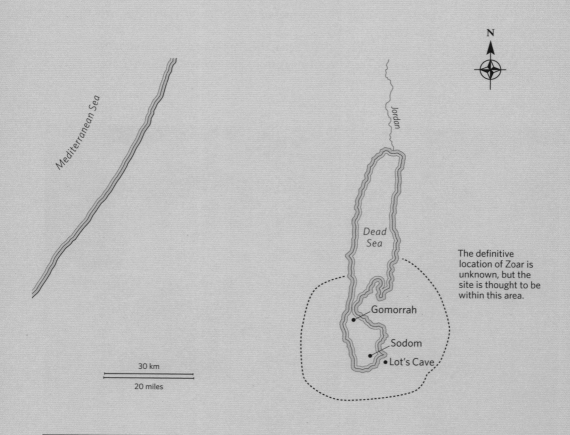

Mediterranean Sea

Jordan

Dead Sea

The definitive location of Zoar is unknown, but the site is thought to be within this area.

Gomorrah

Sodom

Lot's Cave

30 km

20 miles

The people of Sodom had long been in the habit of practising 'abominations', according to the Quran (Book 11) and the Bible (Genesis 13.13). These texts rather coyly avoid telling us what these abominations were, and it was only some two thousand years later that the Christian Church decided that this must be a reference to what it considered the 'sin' of sodomy.

It may in fact be that the main abomination in ancient eyes was the violation of the sacred rites and customs of hospitality. Sodom was notorious for mistreating strangers, as was nearby Gomorrah and other cities in the region of the Dead Sea around the end of the Bronze Age in 1200 BC. Accordingly the Lord, or Allah or Jehovah, dispatched two (or three) angels to Sodom. They took up temporary residence at the house of a man called Lot, whom the Almighty had identified as the one good man in the city. Once word of the divinely handsome strangers got out, a crowd formed outside the house, demanding to 'know' the newcomers. The exact word used, *yada*, has caused some controversy, because wanting to 'know' someone in the intimate sense that *yada* implies might suggest a desire for sex.

Lot seemed to think that the crowd had carnal pleasure in mind, for he informed them, 'Behold now, I have two daughters which have not known man; let me, I pray you, bring them out unto you, and do ye to them as is good in your eyes: only unto these men do nothing; for therefore came they under the shadow of my roof' (Genesis 19.8).

The unfriendly shores of the Dead Sea as seen from the Jordanian side. Located on an active tectonic fault, the sea is subject to earthquakes, and is also one of the saltiest bodies of water in the world.

Disregarding this extraordinary offer, the mob continued to bay for the strangers, until the angels whisked Lot and his family out of town and literally told them to head for the hills. The actions of the mob had doomed Sodom, and also Gomorrah and several other cities, for the patience of the Lord was now exhausted. According to the Quran, Lot's wife remained among the ungodly in Sodom – one might speculate that she had vented strong feelings about her husband's proposal to toss her virgin daughters to the mob.

Fearing he would not make it to the mountains in time, Lot pleaded that instead he might be allowed to shelter in the nearby city of Zoar, and the angel agreed to spare the town. It helped that Zoar was the smallest of those cities scheduled for destruction – indeed, the name of the town translates to something like 'smallest'. 'Then the Lord rained upon Sodom and upon Gomorrah brimstone and fire from the Lord out of heaven; And he overthrew those cities, and all the plain, and all the inhabitants of the cities, and that which grew upon the ground. But his wife looked back from behind him, and she became a pillar of salt' (Genesis 19.26).

Assisted by angels, Lot and his family flee the doomed city of Sodom in this oil painting by Jacob Jacobsz. de Wet, c. 1680.

Three thousand years later, the fact that Zoar survived the catastrophe is considered key to finding Sodom and Gomorrah, as well as Admah and Zeboim, likewise smitten by the wrath of the Lord yet promptly forgotten. The problem is that, although Zoar remained inhabited until the late medieval era, it is also lost.

Zoar before Lot

There are several possible sites, for the Jordan Valley was one of the earliest areas in the world to be settled and is rich in ancient ruins. Even before the catastrophe at Sodom, Zoar was already old. The city was originally called Bela, but it apparently had a name change even before the Hebrews came to dominate the Canaanite culture in the region. The Syriac Chronicles (a collection of texts dating between the sixth and thirteenth centuries AD) describe an ancient tradition of the founding of the 'cities of the plain', which happened two generations before Abraham. A Canaanite called Armonius founded two towns, which he named after his sons Sodom and Gomorrah. A third town he named (or renamed) after his wife Zoara.

When Moses reached the promised land, he is said to have viewed the 'plain of the valley of Jericho, the city of palm trees, unto Zoar' (Deuteronomy 34:3). The 'plain of Jericho' refers not simply to flat land but to a specific area encompassed by the five 'cities of the plain', of which Zoar was by then the only one left standing. The area was also known in the Bible as the Valley of Siddim. It first came to the attention of Hebrew chroniclers when the cities of the plain rebelled against an Elamite king called Chedorlaomer. Chedorlaomer is not referenced in any other source, but so patchy is information from this era that this does not disprove his existence. His name can be translated as 'Servant of Lagamar', a powerful Elamite deity; a Hebrew writer inventing a king would probably not have conformed so accurately to Elamite grammar and nomenclature. Chedorlaomer was driven from the plain by the patriarch Abraham (whom one does not normally think of as a war leader) and the five cities were freed, only to fall into the moral turpitude which led to their destruction.

Before their fall, the cities were reasonably prosperous, partly owing to their location on the Dead Sea. In later years Zoar was said to have produced balsam and indigo, and exported dates from the palm trees that grew in abundance at a nearby oasis – which may have been the reason for the town's location in the first place. In the third century AD the Christian writer Eusebius (*Onomasticon*, 261) described the Dead Sea as lying 'between Jericho and Zoar', and says that remnants of the land's fertility were still discernible. The city

Lot's Cave

1 The original natural cave. Recent finds, including pottery sherds and flint tools, suggest that the cave was first occupied during the Early Bronze Age, *c.* 3000 BC.

2 During the Byzantine period, a monastic site was built around the cave, including a basilica, living quarters for the monks and a hostel for pilgrims. Various inscriptions around the site invoking 'Saint Lot' suggest that the cave was a popular destination for pilgrims.

3 The basilica church was built around the sixth century AD and creates an elaborate entrance to the cave.

4a, b, c In total there are six different mosaic floors at the site, dating from the late sixth and seventh centuries AD.

may also have served as a deep-water port at one end of the Dead Sea (though which end has provoked passionate debate among scholars).

One of the main products of the region was asphalt. In fact, the Dead Sea was known as Asphaltites in antiquity precisely because of this valuable product, which the Roman geographer Strabo (16.2.42) tells us locals would retrieve from the lake in lumps. This very source of wealth was probably the cause of later devastation: it has been speculated that an earthquake caused a massive explosion of asphalt. It may be significant that the ancients considered asphalt to be a type of clay, and that the Quran describes Sodom as being destroyed by a rain of clay tablets (Book 11). Knowledge of this event survived beyond the Abrahamic tradition. In the first century BC Strabo described it thus in his *Geography* (16.2.44):

> Evidence of the fiery nature of the countryside can be seen elsewhere. Near Moasada [not the more famous Masada] the jagged rocks have been scorched, the ground is split and the soil is ashy. Oozing pitch can be smelled from some distance away due to its repugnant odour. There are signs of ruined cities … and the locals frequently claim that … because of earthquakes and fiery eruptions the lake once burst from its banks and the rocks were covered with lava. As for the cities, some were engulfed and others were abandoned by the survivors.

It is also possible that tectonic activity drastically changed the sea level and Sodom and Gomorrah joined the long list of drowned cities.

Zoar after Lot

Zoar survived and went on to be settled largely by the Moabites, a people said to be descended from one of the daughters of Lot. Moab was allegedly conceived when, years after the flight from Sodom and in the absence of any suitable males, the daughters got their father drunk and raped him. The Romans later used Zoar as a way-station, and a unit of native cavalry archers were stationed there. In the late Roman empire the town was a centre of Jewish culture.

One of the most tantalizing pieces of evidence as to Zoar's location is a mosaic, known as the Madaba Map, on the floor of a Byzantine-era church in Jordan. Zoar is clearly shown, but because of changing sea levels and ancient names falling into disuse, the location remains unclear. In the early medieval period Arab writers praised the sweetness of dates from Zoar's oasis, but again have failed to help modern researchers locate the place.

Perhaps the last description of Zoar comes from the English traveller Sir John Mandeville, who visited around 1350, when rising water levels had partly submerged the site (in his *Travels*, 1356):

> Zoar, by the prayer of Lot, was saved and kept a great while, for it was set upon a hill; and yet sheweth thereof some part above the water, and men may see the walls when it is fair weather and clear. Also at the right side of that Dead Sea, dwelleth yet the wife of Lot in likeness of a salt stone.

Zoar Today

After staying in Zoar Lot and his daughters moved to a nearby cave, where Moab was born. Identifying ancient Zoar as the modern settlement of Ghor es-Safi, the Jordanians have turned the nearby 'Cave of Lot' into 'the world's lowest museum', at nearly 400 metres (1,300 feet) below sea level. Whether or not this is Lot's actual cave, the museum shows artefacts from the rich history of the area and its intertwined Jewish, Christian and Arab communities, stretching from the early Bronze Age to the present day, and reminds us that, even if lost these past five hundred years, Zoar lasted a great deal longer than most cities.

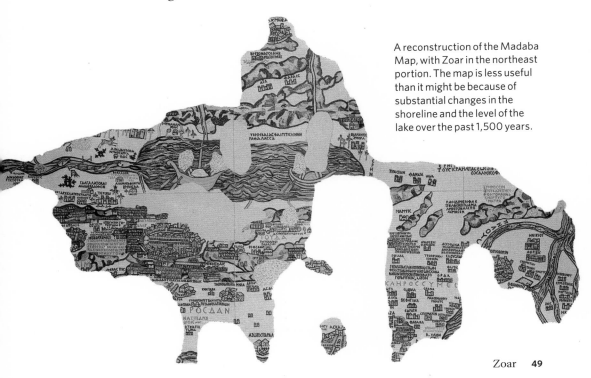

A reconstruction of the Madaba Map, with Zoar in the northeast portion. The map is less useful than it might be because of substantial changes in the shoreline and the level of the lake over the past 1,500 years.

c. 3000–1200 BC
Hattusa
Imperilled Imperial City

If whoever after me becomes king resettles Hattusa,
let the Storm God of the Sky smite him.

Final line of the Proclamation of Anitta

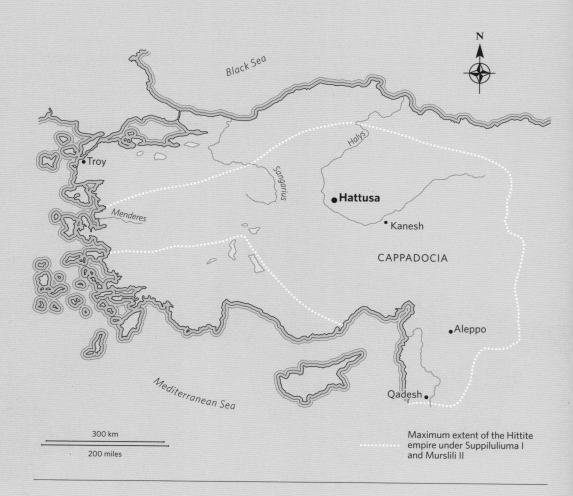

N

Black Sea

Halys

Troy

Sangarius

Hattusa

Menderes

Kanesh

CAPPADOCIA

Aleppo

Mediterranean Sea

Qadesh

300 km

200 miles

Maximum extent of the Hittite
empire under Suppiluliuma I
and Murslili II

The location of the city of Hattusa was both a blessing and – quite literally – a curse. Around 5000 BC the first settlers came to the site, located on the northern central mountain ridge of Anatolia. A rolling plain watered by the Kızılırmak river promised fertile fields, while the wooded slope that gently rose to a knoll on the south side of the plain offered both building materials and protection. It even had water, for a creek ran down the slope into the river. A large nearby forest had abundant timber and plentiful wildlife. In short, given the tendency of humans of the Neolithic era to move into ever-larger settlements, Hattusa was the sort of location that would inevitably become a city sooner or later.

The first settlers were a mysterious people called the Hattians, who settled on the knoll and who had established a small but flourishing city by the start of the Bronze Age. They called their city-state Hattush, and subsisted mainly on barley and einkorn (the type of wheat grown by the first farmers). Meat and clothing were provided by sheep pastured on the plain and – at least in later years – flax and lentils were also cultivated. In short, the Hattians enjoyed all the blessings of nature. Their main problem was their fellow humans, particularly their aggressively expansionist neighbours, a people called the Hittites.

Until recently, historians considered the Hittites a semi-legendary people, rather like the Trojans. The only mentions of the Hittites

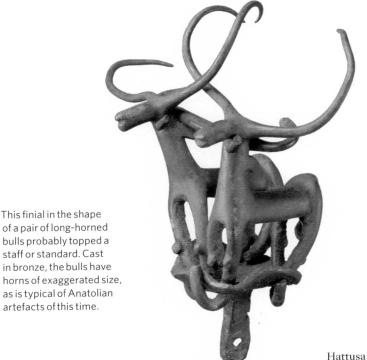

This finial in the shape of a pair of long-horned bulls probably topped a staff or standard. Cast in bronze, the bulls have horns of exaggerated size, as is typical of Anatolian artefacts of this time.

One of six gates into the city, the so-called Lion Gate is partly made of unfinished stone. This suggests that despite the elaborately carved lions flanking the entrance, the gate was never fully completed.

were in the Bible, where they are described as a minor tribe from somewhere in north Syria. Yet, like the Trojans, the Hittites were very real, and important. The Hattians certainly had reason to know where they were (though their city of Kussara is also now lost), and contact between the Hittites of Kussara and Hattians of Hattush was bruising. When the Hittites conquered Hattush around 1700 BC, the Hittite king Anitta ordered the city to be destroyed, weeds to be sown across the site, and a tablet erected demanding that the 'God of Storms' smite any king who attempted to resettle the city.

Yet so ideal was the location that it was only a matter of time before humans moved back onto the ridge. The city was re-founded around a century later by another Hittite king from Kussara called Hattusili, who made what was now called Hattusa his capital. Ironically, the attempt of King Anitta to obliterate Hattusa is only known today thanks to records preserved in that city's archives.

As the Hittites went on to become the dominant power in Asia Minor, Hattusa grew and flourished. The city had always attracted foreign conquerors, and among those who threatened its walls were the Akkadians, the Assyrians and the Egyptians. In fact, currently on display at the United Nations in New York is a copy of the first ever recorded international peace treaty, signed by the Hittites and Ramesses II of Egypt in 1259 BC and discovered at Hattusa.

Those attempting to storm the walls of Hattusa had a tough job, because Hattusa's Hittite kings had boosted the natural defences of the site with walls around 8 metres (26 feet) thick. These stretched more than 6 kilometres (3¾ miles) around the city and had over a hundred defensive towers. By that time, Hattusa was divided into

a higher city, the Büyükkale (Great Fortress), and a lower city which housed most of the population – around fifty thousand people.

The high city had its own additional defensive wall, and contained the royal residence and dozens of temples. It also held a priceless archive of cuneiform tablets, thousands of which (clay tablets being virtually indestructible) have since been excavated. Containing administrative records, legal documents, details of religious ceremonies and Hittite literature, the tablets give us an unprecedented glimpse into the lives of the citizens of Hattusa over three thousand years ago.

This information is supplemented by the efforts of archaeologists, who have discovered gardens, an open-air theatre and large water-storage ponds – one of which seems to have become a rubbish tip, for over a tonne of pottery has been dug out of it so far.

In the mountain range 2 kilometres (about a mile) northeast of Hattusa the Hittite kings established the rock sanctuary of Yazılıkaya, with chambers filled with striking Hittite bas-reliefs showing kings and gods. There is also a huge open-air temple where the kings sacrificed for the well-being of their empire and the imperial city.

Such sacrifices seemed needed, because the climate of the northern highlands was becoming colder and more arid. Some time around 1200 BC Hattusa was temporarily abandoned, and as no signs of looting or pillage have been discovered, it is possible that a natural disaster such as a famine prompted the evacuation. If famine was the cause, it was despite the extraordinary efforts of the Hittite kings. Hattusa had huge granaries, several longer than a football pitch, that had the capacity to hold over 2,000 tonnes of grain.

A changing world had put the once-thriving city in danger. The Hittite empire was in steep decline, riven by political turmoil within and attacks from foreign foes. The end of the Bronze Age brought with it the collapse of civilizations across the Mediterranean world, and the Hittite kingdom was among the casualties. A ferocious warrior people called the Kaskans had long resisted Hittite expansion northward in the area of the Black Sea, and with the weakening of the empire the Kaskans fell upon Hattusa and pillaged and burned it just as Anitta had done a thousand years before. That the city was violently stormed rather than besieged is attested to by huge amounts of charred grain later discovered in the city's warehouses.

Over the following decades the ruins of Hattusa were gradually abandoned. Some 800 years later a small settlement reappeared on the site, which remained as a village until the Byzantine era, when it was once again abandoned. Thereafter both Hattusa, and the Hittite empire of which it had once been the proud capital, were forgotten.

Carved from basalt, this Hittite statuette representing either a priest or a god stands almost a metre (3 feet) high.

The first cuneiform clay tablets at Hattusa were discovered in the 1890s. This example has not travelled far, as it is now only a few kilometres away in the Boğazkale Archaeological Museum, Turkey.

Hattusa Today

Hattusa was rediscovered in the nineteenth century, and since then the site has been continuously excavated. The Turkish authorities have taken great pride in preserving this aspect of their ancient heritage and complain fiercely about ancient artefacts taken from the site by early European explorers.

Of particular contention have been the sphinxes which once adorned the city gates of Hattusa. The sphinx seems to have been a particular emblem of the city and several were discovered in various states of preservation. One such sculpture, which had been on display in the Pergamon Museum in Berlin since 1934, was returned to its home in Turkey in 2011.

Hattusa is now well populated by archaeologists and tourists. One attraction is a reconstructed section of 65 metres (213 feet) of city wall, built with the same techniques and materials as used by the original builders. Visitors can also ponder the significance of a glassy green cube of stone prominently located in one of the temples – the nephrite-type rock was evidently of some significance, but there is no reference to it in any of the ancient sources.

Those looking for relaxation in nature can move on to the İbikçam Forest, the last remnant of the dense forest south of the capital which once made Hattusa such a desirable site for settlers.

c. 2500–600 BC
Mardaman
The Indomitable City

As the decades turned to centuries and millennia, knowledge of Mardaman slipped from human consciousness.

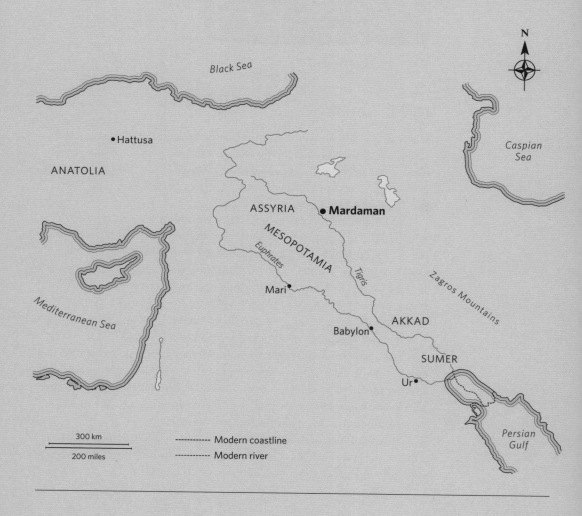

There are tens of thousands of clay cuneiform tablets in museums around the world, and others are still being discovered in Mesopotamia and Anatolia. Certainly more tablets exist than there are people to translate them, so these tablets are only gradually giving up their secrets.

Often these tablets refer to people unknown to history, and to places that have yet to be discovered. For example, they describe a people called the Hurrians who lived in what is now northern Syria, Iraq and eastern Anatolia and worshipped a goddess called Shuwala of Mardaman. We also know of Shuwala from archaeological records in Ur, Hattusa and other cities. All this tells us that, while Shuwala was widely worshipped in the region, she was the primary deity of the city of Mardaman, in rather the same way that Athena was worshipped across the Hellenic world, but particularly in Athens.

But where was Mardaman? From other references it has long been known that Mardaman was a city of considerable importance somewhere in ancient Mesopotamia. Texts from Babylon occasionally name the place, so it must have been a going concern in the second millennium BC. It was probably located on trade routes, because some of the cuneiform tablets that mention the city are commercial in nature.

However, for the first century or so that the city was known to modern scholarship the actual location of Mardaman was a mystery,

Cuneiform tablets are often found fragmented with some of the text damaged. Painstakingly reconstructing the information on such tablets is time-consuming and explains why many tablets have not yet been deciphered.

making it one of around a dozen cities in the region that are known to have survived into the Classical era, but which have subsequently vanished from the historical record.

Yet it seems that someone, over thirty centuries ago, made a conscious decision to preserve the legacy of Mardaman for future generations. Crucial records were stuffed inside a large pottery vessel, and this vessel was covered with a thick layer of clay and buried underground. From the archaeological evidence this happened shortly after the surrounding buildings had been destroyed. Perhaps the intention was that the clay tablets would be unearthed when new buildings were constructed to house them. Instead, they remained buried beside the ruined record hall as the decades turned to centuries and the centuries to millennia, and the knowledge that Mardaman had ever existed slipped from human consciousness.

Enigmatic ruins

In nineteenth-century Europe there was a general reawakening of interest in archaeological discoveries in the ancient 'Near East' – that is, the part that was 'near' to the Western archaeologists who descended in droves to dig the place up, looking for treasures to place in museums at home. Particularly prized were relics from places mentioned in the Bible, as these grounded the Christian religion in established fact.

Assyria was particularly popular in Victorian England, where the discovery of a previously unknown ancient civilization piqued the interest of a people who felt they were establishing a new world order of their own. Numerous settlements in Mesopotamia were discovered and excavated, and others mapped for future exploration. Passing mention was made of a potential site at the village of Bassetki in present-day Kurdish Iraq, but the site was largely overlooked for the nineteenth and most of the twentieth century.

The village was sharply bumped up the archaeological 'to do' list by the discovery of what is known today as the Bassetki Statue – a depiction of the Akkadian king Naram-Sin. The turbulent modern politics of the region made further exploration impossible until, after a few violent wars, Bassetki finally became part of what is (as of 2022) the relatively stable autonomous Kurdish area of Iraq.

Excavations of the area around Bassetki began in earnest after 2010. These revealed a substantial Bronze Age city, at the centre of a road nexus that would have made it a major hub in trade between Mesopotamia and Anatolia. Digging revealed older settlement layers, which pushed the age of the city ever further back into the past until it was determined that humans had been living at the site since the early Bronze Age.

A city wall was discovered, a palace and a residential district. All this evidence pointed to a city of considerable importance in the ancient world, but no-one knew what that city was. Until those carefully buried records were finally unearthed.

Pictures of the crumbling clay tablets were sent to Dr Betina Faist, an Assyrian-language specialist at the University of Heidelberg. Her studies opened a window into the rich history of the city and finally, in 2019, revealed that the ruins were those of the lost city of Mardaman.

Conquest, reconquest and re-reconquest

Much is now known about the city – it repeatedly faced adversity, and rose and fell several times in its storied career. At some periods it belonged to different empires, and at others it achieved a precarious independence from the great powers that struggled for dominance in the region.

The story started around 2800 BC, when what was to be Mardaman developed as a stopping place along the trade routes

Another city bites the dust: British artist John Martin's take on the fall of Nineveh, another Assyrian city of Upper Mesopotamia. Though evocative, the painting is largely based on the artist's imagination, as the first excavations at Nineveh did not begin until twelve years later, in 1842.

that were becoming established between cities such as Ur in Mesopotamia and others in Anatolia. By the time of the Third Dynasty of Ur (*c.* 2200–2000 BC) we find mentions of the city as a trade nexus.

By then, there was already a substantial wall around the city, but this did not save it from conquest. In fact, the first time that the name of Mardaman crops up in the written record is a mention of its destruction at the hands of Naram-Sin – the king whose statue aroused modern interest in Bassetki in the first place.

It seems that at this time the city was already part of the Akkadian empire, but under a ruler called Duhsusu it took part in the so-called Great Revolt against Akkadian rule and struck out for independence. In response, Naram-Sin crushed both the revolt and the city of Mardaman.

Mardaman was rebuilt, and after the fall of Akkad it seems to have become a part of the kingdom of Mittani, ruled by the little-known Hurrian people. It is at this point that Shuwala became the city's protecting deity, though from subsequent evidence it would appear that the goddess performed rather poorly in that role.

Cuneiform was written with a triangular nib pressed into wet clay. Once the clay was baked it could be shattered, but not destroyed. This fragment is shown alongside a terracotta figurine from the city's Mittani period (1600–1350 BC).

We next hear of Mardaman when it was reconquered again, this time by the Assyrian king Shamshi-Adad I, who briefly folded the city into his rising empire in 1786 BC. As Assyrian power temporarily waned, Mardaman tried to strike out as an independent kingdom once more. It promptly fell out with the nearby city of Mari, and records from that city tell of Mardaman being conquered yet again, this time by Mari's allies.

Some time thereafter the warlike Turukkaean people descended from the nearby Zagros mountains and razed the city. However, Mardaman rose yet again, along with the resurgent Assyrian empire. By 1250 BC Mardaman was a provincial capital, ruled by an Assyrian governor named Assur-nasir. The record is particularly good for this period, because the rediscovered tablets record the life of Mardaman a generation before it was flattened again, this time around 1200 BC, the point at which the clay records containing the city's story were buried.

Who took this particular turn at destroying Mardaman, and why, is uncertain, for at this point the written record ends. However, archaeologists have determined that the indomitable city rose once more in the Neo-Assyrian era, and enjoyed a final flowering around 900–600 BC. Yet again, though, the fate of Mardaman was linked to the fate of the Assyrian empire. When Assyria was destroyed by rebellion and civil war, so too was Mardaman. By now trade routes had changed, and in the Iron Age new commodities took different routes to market. There was no point in rebuilding the ancient city and the ruins were abandoned. In the end, commerce did what successive conquerors had failed to do, and removed Mardaman from the map.

Mardaman Today

Few things excite archaeologists more than a rediscovered lost city, so the site is now being enthusiastically excavated. However, unlike their nineteenth-century counterparts, who were often little better than treasure-hunters, modern archaeologists are a slow, methodical species seeking information rather than riches. Located in an area suitable for only the most intrepid of tourists, the city has been so recently rediscovered that much of its history and geography will remain for decades a mystery to the casual visitor.

c. 3500 BC–AD 100
Thebes
The Pride of Egypt

Egyptian Thebes where the piled ingots gleam.

Homer, *Iliad* IX.382

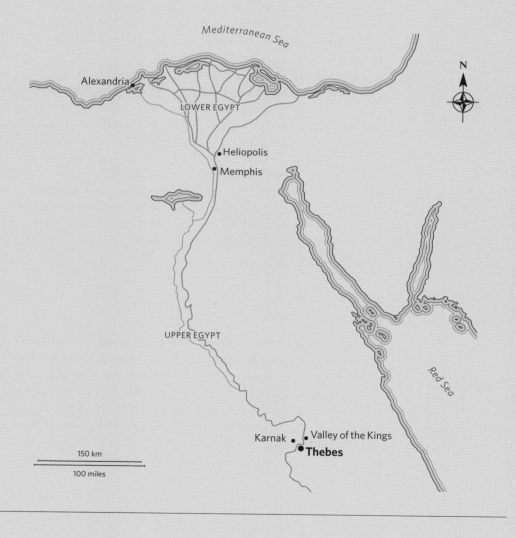

An aerial view of the Ramesseum – a temple built by Ramesses II to enshrine his legacy. The shattered statue of Ramesses within is said to have inspired Percy Bysshe Shelley's famous poem 'Ozymandias' (Ozymandias was the Greeks' name for Ramesses).

Waset had been a political and religious centre in Egypt for over a thousand years before the first Greeks visited the city. This they probably did in the Mycenaean era (1700–1050 BC) and they were greatly impressed by the city's temple complex at Karnak, which had been founded hundreds of years earlier. Consequently, the Greeks referred to the city as 'the temple' – *Thebai*. This misidentification has proven impossible to eradicate from Western culture and even today the lost Egyptian city is usually referred to by the name 'Thebes' rather than its Egyptian name of 'Waset'.

There is some dispute as to where the name Waset comes from, not least because the city was established well before Egyptian was standardized as a language. What 'Waset' meant in the original local dialect is anyone's guess. It has been speculated that the name refers to the *was*, a sceptre traditionally carried by the pharaoh, though this would have required remarkably forward thinking from the original pre-pharaonic inhabitants. The settlement was originally founded around 3500 BC, when Egypt was not yet ruled by a single king.

Certainly Waset was among the very first Egyptian cities. It lay on the alluvial plain created by silt deposited on a sweeping bend of the Nile, and was probably formed by the coalescence of smaller villages. Sited some 800 kilometres (500 miles) south of the Nile delta, the area was naturally rich farmland. This location also made the new town a natural site for trade between the tribal clans of the south and the more settled north.

The first written records of the city are from hieroglyphs dated to around 2600 BC. By then the rulers of Thebes had expanded their domain considerably. One of the first on record was Intef I, who ruled Thebes late in the twenty-second century BC. Intef was not an Egyptian pharaoh in the traditional later sense, but appears to have been lord of a considerable tract of land, from Aswan in the far south to the city of Coptos, some 43 kilometres (26 miles) north of Thebes.

The increasing importance of Thebes saw a commensurate rise in the status of the city's principal deity, the god Amun. By the start of the second millennium BC Amun had become identified with the sun god Ra and was acknowledged across most of Egypt as the king of the gods. This gave further importance to Thebes as the centre of Amun's worship, and the temple sites on the west bank began to expand to assume a national role. From the Bible (e.g. Ezekiel 30:14)

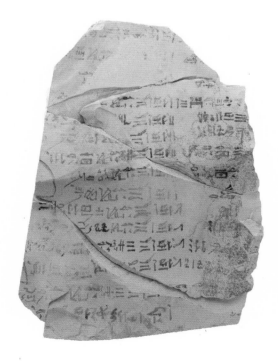

In the ancient world pottery sherds, or *ostraca*, were used for messages and note-taking. This example is from Egypt in the 20th Dynasty (c. 1100 BC).

we know that the Hebrews called Thebes 'No[-Amon]' – the city of Amun.

Around 1700–1550 BC a wind blew in from the north, carrying with it the ships of a mysterious people called the Hyksos. From whence they originated is still uncertain, but they had superior military technology and the northern part of the country gradually fell under their sway.

This ill wind for Egypt was good for Thebes, which quickly became the main centre of resistance to the invaders and the capital of the rulers of the 13th Dynasty (it had previously been the capital of Intef's 11th Dynasty, before power shifted northwards). It took generations for the Theban-based rulers to drive out the Hyksos, and by that time Thebes was incontestably the main city of Egypt. Indeed by then Thebes, with a population of some 60,000 people, may have become the largest city in the world.

Trade now flowed not only down the Nile, but also across the desert. Caravans came with goods from India and Punt (thought to be the coastal area of modern Ethiopia). Later, a port was to be built at Myos Hormos (modern al-Quoseir) on the Red Sea to handle this traffic, which the geographer Strabo put at well over a hundred ships a day. At this time trade also began with a people to the north called the Hellenes, who were to base much of their newly evolving culture upon the Egyptian model.

Under the king Ramesses II (1279–1213 BC), Egypt reached the height of its power. Thebes itself could be said to have peaked somewhat earlier, as Ramesses moved his capital north to a purpose-built city in the Nile delta. The new location made it easier for Ramesses to fight his wars in Mediterranean lands. Nevertheless, Thebes continued to thrive as a religious centre – not least because of the continued patronage of Ramesses, who had the temples of the city rebuilt on a grander and more splendid scale.

When Homer, in the eighth century BC, referred in the *Iliad* to 'Egyptian Thebes where the piled ingots gleam', the other Thebes, in Greece, was hardly a rival – the Greeks themselves distinguished between 'Thebes of the Hundred Gates' in Egypt and 'Seven-gated Thebes' in Boeotia. The much-travelled historian Herodotus (*c.* 484–420 BC) claims to have visited Thebes in Egypt and talked with the priests there, who told him of the Theban origins of Dodona, a famed oracle of Zeus in northwestern Greece.

Yet the glory of Egyptian Thebes was nearing its end. The very location in the south which had protected the city from the Hyksos made Thebes vulnerable to the Kushites, who attacked from the opposite direction (modern Sudan).

Three massive terraces form the impressive memorial temple of Hatshepsut, *c*.1425 BC. Among the few female pharaohs of Egypt, Hatshepsut was a prolific builder, and this temple is generally considered her masterwork.

The Kushite conquerors became the 25th Dynasty of Egypt (747–656 BC). It was the first time the whole country had come under foreign rule. The civilizations to the north took note, and in 663 BC Ashurbanipal of Assyria launched a devastating raid from which Thebes never really recovered. Later, Ashurbanipal would boast that he had stripped the 'wealth of the palaces, cloths, linen, precious stones' and two obelisks of electrum weighing 2,500 talents (a whopping 62,500 kilograms, approximately; the exact weight of an Assyrian talent is uncertain). Further conquests were to come. First the Persians attacked and added Egypt to their empire in 525 BC, and then Alexander the Great defeated the Persians and Egypt came under the rule of Ptolemaic (Greek) rulers, the last of whom was Cleopatra VII.

Memory of past glories made Thebes a sullenly nationalistic rival to the Greek capital of Egypt in Alexandria, and several rebellions against Ptolemaic rule were centred around the city. The Ptolemies responded by giving more power and autonomy to the priestly castes in Thebes, but the city remained in decline. By the time the Romans defeated Cleopatra and made Egypt a Roman province in 30 BC, mighty Thebes was barely a shadow of its former self, with a population that lived partly by farming and partly by entertaining Roman tourists who came to see the famed ruins. One reported: 'The city has been abandoned and there are several temples, but most of these, too, were mutilated ... and now Thebes is only a collection of villages' (Strabo, *Geography* 17.1.46).

Thebes Today

Now going under the name of Luxor, Thebes has revived, partly on the back of a thriving tourist trade. The site contains so many monuments and temples that it has been fittingly and frequently described as the world's largest museum. These attractions include the temple complex at Karnak, the famed tombs of the Valley of the Kings, and the great temples of the Ramesseum and of queen Hatshepsut at Deir el-Bahari. As with many ancient cities, the area is now a UNESCO World Heritage Site.

A Theban obelisk was taken by the emperor Constantius II (r. AD 337–361) to serve as a decoration at the Circus Maximus in Rome. The toppled remains were restored in the sixteenth century and now stand outside the Lateran Palace. At 25 metres (over 80 feet) in height, the Theban obelisk is taller than its more famed rival from Heliopolis, which stands at the entrance to St Peter's Square at the Vatican.

Opposite Stele from Thebes. These flat stone slabs were used in the ancient world to commemorate people or special occasions. This was commissioned by one Luef-er-bak, 'guardian of the store-house of the Temple of Amun'. The carving shows him (right) with his wife and adult children.

c. 3500–300 BC
Phaistos
Second City of Minoan Crete

It may have lacked a labyrinth or a Minotaur,
but the city had other advantages.

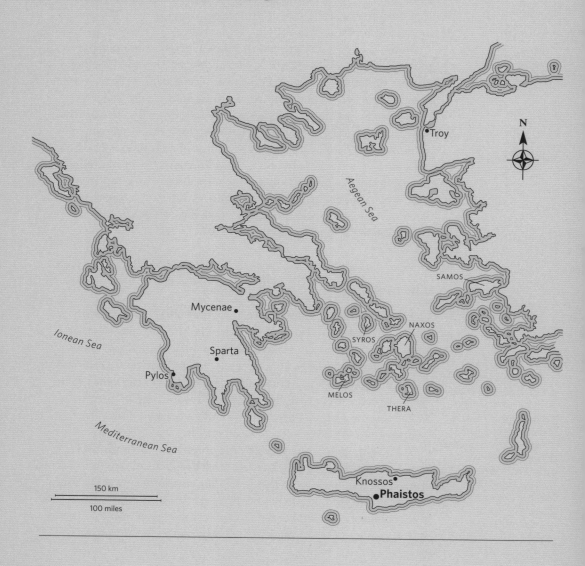

The so-called Minoan civilization in Crete began around 5000 BC, proving that the ancient Greeks were wrong to assume that the father of Cretan civilization was King Minos (who lived three generations before the Trojan War, around 1300 BC). Therefore, we can also safely rule out the Greek theory that Phaistos, one of the first large Minoan cities, was established by Rhadamanthus, the brother of Minos.

Phaistos was some 96 kilometres (60 miles) from King Minos's palace at Knossos. It may have lacked a labyrinth or a Minotaur, but the city had other advantages. Phaistos was located in central Crete, about 5 kilometres (3 miles) from the sea, where a high ridge separates the inland Messara plain from the coastal Debaki plain. Whoever founded Phaistos probably chose the location not just for the view, but because it controlled both fertile agricultural plains and the Geropotamos river.

That said, the view from Phaistos is probably the most spectacular in Crete, and the palace builders made the most of dramatic vistas

Phaistos had some of the best views of any city in ancient Crete. This view of the site shows how, through its strategic location, Phaistos dominated the agricultural lands below.

of the Messara plain, framed by the Asterousia mountain range and the Lasithi plateau.

The earliest structures at the site date back to around 3500 BC, in the Late Neolithic era, but the city's spectacular rise to prominence began around five hundred years later, after which time Phaistos was probably second only to Knossos in wealth and splendour.

The name we give to the city today is a Greekified version of the Minoan original, because the Greeks associated the city with one Phaistos, a grandson of Hercules. The original name probably exists on one of the written fragments that archaeologists have excavated from the ruins, but the writing comes in two forms – Linear A, which remains undeciphered, and Cretan hieroglyphs, which make Linear A look easy.

Once Phaistos had become one of the leading cities of the leading civilization west of Egypt, an unknown ruler and architect set about building a palatial complex worthy of the city's status. A huge amount of work went into the construction. Three massive terraces were excavated high on the hillside so that the palace would overlook the town where the ordinary citizens lived. (This town is only now beginning to get some attention from archaeologists.)

The Greeks of the Mycenaean and Archaic eras were familiar with Phaistos and Homer mentions it several times, describing it as 'well-situated'. He also says that the Phaistians supplied ships as part of the fleet that invaded Troy, and ten years later some of the returning fleet were wrecked on the southern shores of Crete nearest to Phaistos.

In the Trojan War Phaistos was on the Greek side, as was Poseidon, god of earthquakes and the sea. Despite this, Poseidon was never kind to the city, for around 1700 BC the splendid palace complex was wrecked by two earthquakes in quick succession. The palace was rebuilt, incorporating several surviving structures from the original, but the replacement was never quite as good.

Nevertheless, the builders were able to make use of the little Geropotamos river that runs down the ridge. They incorporated this river into the palace's sewers, giving the complex a sanitation system that would have been the envy of medieval castles built two-and-a-half millennia later. The addition of several deep wells sunk within the palace grounds guaranteed a secure water supply for the inhabitants.

Even today the remains of the palace are impressive. There is a large theatre which could accommodate four hundred people (five hundred if they were very friendly), although the splendid view from the seating area must have distracted many viewers from the stage.

The palace also had large storerooms, containing the characteristic large oil jars that are a feature of Minoan palaces. Another distinctive feature found at Phaistos is a type of pottery called Kamares Ware. Coloured white, orange and red, Kamares cups and jars mostly have marine or floral motifs. The pottery is thinner and more delicate than average, with some cups barely thicker than an eggshell. Interestingly, no Kamares Ware has been found outside Minoan palaces, which suggests that its use was restricted to the elite.

Regrettably Poseidon was not finished with the palace at Phaistos, and in 1600 BC the place was once more so severely damaged by an earthquake that the builders had to start all over again. It was worth it, because the advantageous position of the city in central Crete made Phaistos still one of the dominant cities on the island – although there are hints that there was already friction with the growing power of the nearby city-state of Gortyn. There was also now a Mycenaean settlement called Agia Triada, which was the first to challenge the dominance of Phaistos and then overtake it.

Things got worse around 1400 BC when the warlike Achaeans (Greeks) attacked Knossos, the main Minoan city. They also sacked the palace at Phaistos. This time the palace was not rebuilt, though the lower city continued to be occupied. In fact the town of Phaistos enjoyed a brief renaissance in the seventh century BC and appears to have remained a going concern for the next four hundred years. Coins apparently struck by the city have motifs featuring mythological characters such as Zeus, Hercules and Europa, with the name of the city on the obverse.

However, by this time Phaistos was no longer the power that it had once been, and it eventually fell victim to the increasingly violent inter-city wars which wracked the island. The final blow was struck in the third century BC by the city's long-standing rival, Gortyn. The ancient geographer Strabo baldly sums up the city's fate. 'Phaestus [Phaistos] was razed to the ground by the Gortynians ... and the country is now held by those who razed it' (Strabo, *Geography* 10.4.14).

Phaistos Today

Phaistos was rediscovered in the late nineteenth century by explorers who used Strabo's description to locate the ruins. Excavations started there even before archaeological work at the more famous Knossos began to reveal the lost Minoan culture to the modern world.

Perhaps the most intriguing discovery from Phaistos is a clay tablet, some 16 centimetres (6 inches) across, which has been facetiously described as 'the world's first CD-ROM'. As with any CD, the information on the disc is laid out in a spiral, though it is not certain whether the spiral should be read from the centre to the rim or the other way around. The disc is in the famously impenetrable Minoan language and contains hundreds of symbols printed into the surface by miniature stamps, depicting things like crocuses, axe-heads, animal pelts and dolphins.

There is considerable academic debate as to what the disc says and how it should be read. The most probable interpretation, based on the little that is known of the language, is that it is a prayer to the 'Great Goddess', though the full content may be as spectacular as an end-of-the-world prophecy or as mundane as a laundry list. Until the language can be deciphered, the Phaistos disc will remain one of the most tantalizing mysteries from the lost city.

Phaistos remains second to Knossos when it comes to visitors on the tourist trail, though that may be an advantage. Whereas the high traffic at Knossos means that many parts of the site have to be roped off to preserve them, the remains at Phaistos are more accessible.

Either daffodils or lilies sprout from this elaborate Kamares-style clay bowl of about 1800 BC. This was probably used during formal occasions or banquets at an aristocratic house in Phaistos.

PART TWO

From Troy to Rome

Well before the start of the Roman era, the ancient world already had an abundance of cities that had been abandoned for one reason or another. A changing climate had made places such as Ur in Mesopotamia unattractive, and more dramatic disasters, such as floods and earthquakes, had accounted for others. Occasionally a city had simply served its purpose, and shifting trade routes or the presence of a more attractive nearby city sucked the population away from an older rival. The dawning of the Iron Age in Europe was to see yet more dramatic changes.

Four thousand years ago, when humanity had about 0.06% of its present numbers, there were already problems arising from overpopulation. This was because overpopulation can be considered not as an absolute number of people but as the ratio of available resources to the size of a given population. The ancient world was considerably less efficient than the modern in extracting, exploiting and sharing resources, so in antiquity scarcity was a fact of life.

There were different solutions available for resolving the issue of scarcity. One was trade, by which people exchanged what they had for those things which they desired to have. If they had few natural resources to trade, they used manufactured goods instead. This in turn boosted the already growing trend towards urbanism, since manufacturers need markets, both to buy raw materials and to sell finished goods.

Another way to resolve the issue of scarcity was to take what was needed from those too weak to prevent it. Consequently, humanity became organized for warfare – for the simple reason that those societies that did not optimize for conflict quickly became extinct at the hands of those who did. Again, cities needed to adapt, which generally involved participation in this regressive human development.

In this era it was no longer enough for a city to be located in a fertile region or on a good trade route (or both, where possible). Now a city also had to be defensible. Between the end of the Bronze Age and the era of imperial Rome, urban history is in part the story of an arms race between those who strove to make cities stronger and better fortified, and those developing new technologies and techniques to overcome those fortifications. In this period some thriving and prosperous cities died out, not because they became obsolete through changing climate or varying patterns of trade, but because they were incapable of defending themselves from a larger, more powerful rival.

The dawn of empire

Cities and states of the era also reflect another transition of humanity – from civil society to enterprise society. Roughly speaking, the mission of a civil society (such as most of the first cities) is for large numbers of humans to live together without killing one another.

An enterprise society develops when enough people in a society decide that, having achieved the first objective – a civil society – they should now use their collective unity to *do* something.

This may be glorifying their gods, building pyramids or a great wall, or – a popular choice – conquering and/or eliminating the neighbours. Collectively, organized cities provided the warehouses, the workers, the fighters and the administrative machinery to achieve these objectives.

Yet there were also positive aspects. The advantages of urbanism and statehood meant that more people lived longer and more peaceful lives than before, and their lives could be much richer. Cities were cultural centres with theatres and sports arenas, and a class of artists, sculptors, playwrights and poets. Artists needed patrons and a venue to display their work, and performers needed an audience. Much as they might rhapsodize about the joys of a bucolic existence, the ancient poets and playwrights were largely an urban phenomenon.

The Mediterranean of the early Classical era had an abundance of urban cultures – as well as the Greeks there were the Phoenicians, Etruscans, Hebrews and Gauls (the latter spent the last two centuries of their independence urbanizing rapidly). However, their cities were what we might consider as 'stand-alone' entities. That is, while a city's inhabitants might have felt they belonged to a nation, the members of that nation felt little need to coordinate politically. Indeed, intra-national warfare was a feature of the pre-Classical era. (The Greeks are an excellent example of this.)

Previously, the only large multi-city empires had lain to the east, with the Egyptians, Hittites, Assyrians and latterly the Persians. The cities of these eastern empires often changed hands, but were seldom destroyed. Now, as the concept of empire was adopted by the expansionist enterprise culture of the Romans, cities such as Carthage or Numantia that stood against the tide were swiftly overwhelmed.

Both the Persians in the east and the Romans in the west realized the benefits of linking their cities with an extensive road network. While these roads were primarily intended for the swift passage of armies, they had the not-incidental benefit of expanding trade networks even further. Resources could be moved more quickly between cities, and also between empires. This era saw massive growth in that extensive network of trade routes known today as the 'Silk Road', and the corresponding rise of caravan cities. These provided not only facilities for merchants bringing goods westward, but also markets where the goods were sold – very few merchants accompanied their wares from start to finish. Most commodities were sold on, with the cities along the way benefiting from taxes on each sale.

Whether a city thrived or fell into decay now depended not only on its individual situation, but also on its role in the overall political entity of which it was a part. Rome's empire expanded quickly, and (although most of the population remained rural) Roman culture was largely urban: Roman expansion would create more cities than it destroyed.

c. 3000–1150 BC
Troy
A Tale of Nine Cities

The kingdom of Troy shall rise again.
Endure and hold out for better days.

Virgil, *Aeneid* 1.205

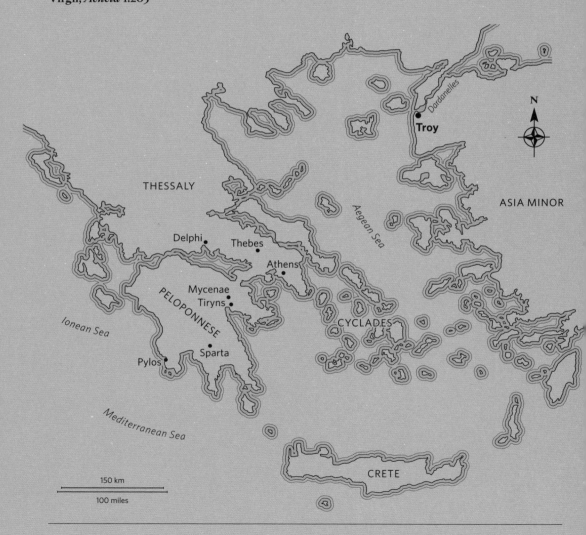

THESSALY

Dardanelles

Troy

ASIA MINOR

Aegean Sea

Delphi Thebes

Athens

Mycenae

Tiryns

PELOPONNESE

CYCLADES

Ionean Sea

Sparta

Pylos

Mediterranean Sea

CRETE

150 km

100 miles

No lost city is more famous than Troy – not because Troy was larger or richer than any other, but because it was the backdrop to one of the seminal works of Western literature, the *Iliad* of Homer.

The *Iliad* tells of a turbulent fortnight in the ten-year Greek siege of Troy, which ultimately led to the sacking and destruction of the city. Yet even as generation after generation read the story of the Trojan War, the actual location of Troy became vaguer and vaguer, until finally it was assumed that Troy, like the heroes and gods who had battled beneath its walls, was totally a figment of myth.

Then, in the late nineteenth century, the amateur archaeologist Heinrich Schliemann announced not only that Troy was a real city in present-day Turkey, but also that he had discovered it. Since then the site has been thoroughly examined by archaeologists, and it has been established that there was not one Troy but at least nine – and Schliemann's Troy was not the Troy of Homer's *Iliad*.

In the Classical era Troy received tourists such as Alexander the Great and, in AD 124, the Roman emperor Hadrian, who renovated the Odeon at the site – shown here – and may even have had his poetry recited there. (Hadrian was quite a good poet.)

The first Troys

Troy was around long before the Trojan War. The first humans to settle on the site did so some five thousand years ago. They chose the western end of a ridge on a fertile plain between two rivers, which are known today as the Karamenderes and the Dumrek Su. This was around the time that the first city-states were getting organized in Mesopotamia, and when Egypt had only just become a single state from an untidy collection of minor kingdoms.

Troy I was a small settlement, with some twenty houses enclosed by a defensive wall of unworked stone. Doubtless the total population was larger than this would suggest, for 'Troy' was a citadel to which the rural population who lived and worked on the plain would flee in times of peril. Little is known of these first Trojans, except that their pottery and metalwork was similar to that of contemporary peoples in northern Anatolia and the islands just off the coast.

Panorama with the Abduction of Helen Amidst the Wonders of the Ancient World, Maerten van Heemskerck, 1535. This art piece is a sort of picture puzzle that challenges viewers to pick out classical sites and references. For example, the rainbow in the background identifies the goddess Iris, who broke the news of the abduction to Helen's husband.

How and why this first settlement was abandoned or destroyed is uncertain, but the site was almost immediately reoccupied. Rather than remove the ruins of the old city, the new settlers simply levelled the debris and built on top of it – a process that happened again and again. Sometimes individual buildings, rather than the entire city, were replaced in this way, so in some parts of Troy there are up to forty-five levels of settlement.

Peak Troy

The earliest settlers were doubtless attracted because the plain offered a good source of food, but as human civilization developed it became clear that Troy was also well placed to become a commercial centre. The city became an important stop on the trade route from Anatolia to the European side of the Dardanelles, and its location at the narrowest point of the Dardanelles gave it command of the sea route between the Aegean Sea and what we now call the Black Sea.

The Trojans were famous horse-breeders – Hector in the *Iliad* is often called 'horse-taming Hector' – and archaeology has supported myth by discovering a substantial number of equine bones in and around Troy.

By 2500 BC Troy was a major city of the Mediterranean-wide Bronze Age civilization. At this point the city's defences had been substantially upgraded, and the citadel now possessed a wall consisting of large blocks of dressed stone bulked up with clay bricks. In this, the city was not unlike many Greek cities of the early Mycenaean culture in Greece, and indeed the fortress area contained buildings of the 'megaron' style found in places such as Mycenae.

Yet the only evidence we have of who was living in Troy at this time is a single bit of writing upon a 5-centimetre-wide (2-inch) seal. The language is Luwian, which connects Troy with a people of the Hittite empire that flourished around 1750 BC. Hittite records refer to the city of Wilusa, which is almost certainly Troy. There are clear etymological links between the name Wilusa and 'Ilium', which is what the early Greeks called Troy (and why Homer's story is called the *Iliad*). Furthermore, the defensive towers of the fortress were square-built to a pattern familiar to archaeologists who have excavated other Hittite cities.

This version of Troy was destroyed by an earthquake around 1300 BC, or if we prefer the more colourful version of myth, by an irate Hercules who was refused payment by the Trojan king for services rendered. The city was rebuilt almost immediately (by Apollo and Poseidon, according to myth), and even larger and better – though showing a decided inclination towards strong defence.

Troy of the *Iliad*

The sixth iteration of Troy (by now fires and earthquakes had taken the city through Troys I–V) is probably closest to the fabled Troy of myth. Certainly the archaeological remains fit Homer's description of 'strongly built' and 'well-walled' Troy, though its legendary 'topless towers' were in fact capped at a still impressive 12 metres (39 feet). Sitting upon already substantial walls, these towers would have afforded an excellent view of the Trojan plain. From one such tower, Paris shot the poisoned arrow that hit Achilles in the heel and killed him.

While we have no contemporary account of the famed siege of Troy (Homer's epic was written half a millennium later), the written record does speak of considerable tension and sometimes open warfare between the Greeks and the Hittites at this time. Certainly around 1250 BC some people felt strongly enough to leave a goodly number of bronze spearheads, arrowheads and slingshot pellets embedded in the mud-brick walls of Troy – which was destroyed shortly thereafter.

Large clay pots buried up to the neck in the ground were evidently meant to contain grain, perhaps showing that the fortress was braced for a siege; skeletons unburied in the streets suggest that this defence was unsuccessful. In short, there are indications that not only the location of Troy but also the story of the *Iliad* is founded upon fact.

The Olympian gods were deeply interested in the fate of Troy, with Hermes and Athena supporting the Greeks in their siege while Artemis (centre) took the Trojans' side. Black-figure vase, c. 600 BC.

After Achilles

The Arrival of Helen in Troy, by the so-called Sienese Master, c.1430. Helen and Paris were delayed in their homecoming by bad weather, which took them to Egypt and elsewhere. However, they were not so delayed as to turn up in the Renaissance dress and ships shown here.

Troy was rebuilt soon after this latest convulsion. There is evidence that the city was attacked again around 1200 BC, but it is unlikely that the attackers were Mycenaean Greeks, as their civilization was in freefall towards collapse at this point. It is more probable that Troy fell victim to the same sort of attackers that destroyed Mycenae and cities in Anatolia – that is, peoples dispossessed by the tumult of the Bronze Age collapse who were looking to share the pain with anyone who had something worth looting.

Thereafter Troy was abandoned until the revival of civilization in the Archaic era of Greece. Settlers renamed their city Ilion, and for centuries it was little more than a village. However, the name of Troy loomed large in the consciousness of the Greeks and later the Romans, particularly as the latter had convinced themselves that they were descended from the Trojan hero Aeneas. Troy became one of the world's first tourist-based economies, and for a while flourished as never before.

In the later Roman empire Troy was considered as the site for a 'New Rome', but Roman engineers looked dubiously at the decaying harbour and opted for Constantinople instead. Wisely, as it turned out: as the coastline changed Troy's harbour continued to silt up, and the city is now 5 kilometres (3 miles) from the sea. A series of earthquakes demolished much that remained of the city.

Troy became a village in the early medieval era, then an abandoned ruin, a legend and finally a myth. All that remained was the mound upon which successive generations had raised their walls. The locals called this Hisarlık.

Troy Today

Troy was rediscovered by a local farmer who knew his myths. He noted that Mount Ida overlooked Hisarlık just as that mountain was said to overlook Troy, and that the site lay between two rivers which may once have been the Scamander and Simois of the *Iliad*.

These observations were enough for noted amateur archaeologist Heinrich Schliemann to investigate the site from 1870. Plunging straight through the Troy VI layer, which modern researchers believe was most likely the city of the *Iliad*, Schliemann found a cache of weapons, gold and jewelry from a thousand years earlier, which he wrongly proclaimed was 'the treasure of Priam'.

Since then Troy has once again become a major tourist attraction, and also an active archaeological dig. The estimated size of the city has been greatly increased by the discovery of a lower town on the landward side of the fortress. This housed the majority of the population and was surrounded by a deep defensive ditch – just as Homer reported.

Today a UNESCO World Heritage Site, Troy boasts a museum opened in 2018 to accommodate hundreds of visitors to the ruins every day. A (slightly kitschy) 12-metre (40-foot) wooden horse stands just outside the site. So far nobody has proposed taking it within.

1200–200 BC
Thonis
The City That Sank Itself

To this port came a runaway couple – Paris and Helen of Troy – blown south by the prevailing winds.

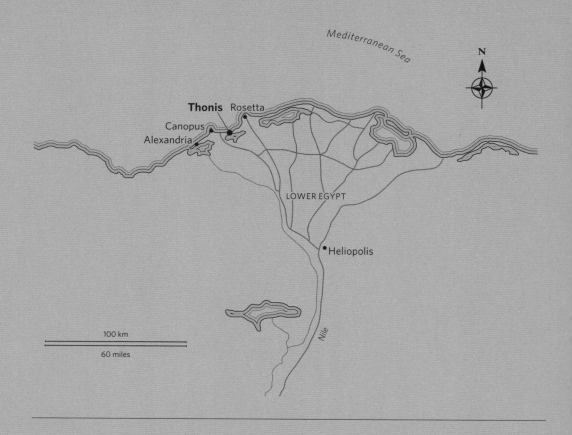

The ancient Greek writer Herodotus (*c.* 484–420 BC) is sometimes called 'the father of history', but because of his habit of retelling fantastical tales that he picked up on his travels he is also sometimes called 'the father of lies'. Two examples of this have been seen in his reports from Egypt – a nation the Greeks knew well from the start of their history.

First, he refers to a type of cargo boat which he calls a *baris*, made from planks of wood from the acacia thorn tree, with overlapping layers laid on the hulls, rather as one might lay bricks. When no such boat was ever located among the numerous marine shipwrecks of the era, marine archaeologists concluded that Herodotus had simply got it wrong.

Second, Herodotus mentions a 'mythical' harbour at the mouth of the Nile where he claims 'there was upon the shore, as still there is now, a temple of Heracles [Hercules]' (*Histories* 2.113). To this place came a runaway couple – Paris and Helen of Troy – blown south by the prevailing winds as they fled from Greece. The 'warden of the

Underwater Osiris. This figurine, made between the fourth and second centuries BC, stands on the seabed, with the vanished city around it.

Nile mouth, whose name was Thonis' was unsure what to do with the pair, but it was eventually decided that the affairs of the Greeks were nothing to do with the Egyptians so long as trade between the two nations continued to flow smoothly. It was assumed for a long time that Thonis and his harbour were an invention of Herodotus. After all, if one is telling the story of Helen of Troy, does one more mythical detail matter?

The real Thonis

The port city was real, however, and trade was its lifeblood. The Greeks called it Herakleion, after the famed temple of Hercules at the site, while the Egyptians used the native name of Thonis. These dual names suited a city which was almost as much Greek as it was Egyptian. The Egyptians preferred that trading with Greeks be done at the designated ports of Naucratis and Thonis, not in the interior of the country.

During the fourth century BC the pharaoh Nectanebo I (r. 380–362 BC) imposed a 10 per cent tax on Greek goods entering Thonis, with the proceeds to go to a temple. 'Let a tithe be given of the gold, the silver, the timber, of the worked wood and anything else from across the sea of the Hau-Nebut [the Mediterranean] as offerings to my divine mother Neith', reads an inscription on the Nectanebo Stele.

From evidence at Naucratis we know that the Greeks not only sold timber to the Egyptians but also silver, copper, wine and olive oil. In return they picked up papyrus, spices and fine Egyptian pottery, with its distinctive faience glaze. Thonis itself was the Venice of its day, a series of islands linked by bridges and split by watercourses. The main islet to the north held the temple of Hercules. There was a series of wharves for shipping, pontoons across the river mouth, and a large canal traversing the islet. Sometimes ship anchors snagged, or captains in a hurry simply abandoned their anchors, leaving hundreds of them in the river silt for later archaeologists to find.

Over seventy shipwrecks littered the harbour floor, dating from between the sixth and second centuries BC. At least some of these were sunk deliberately: as a defensive measure, as part of rituals, or simply because the port authorities wanted to use them as the foundation for land reclamation and further building.

Thonis was the main port of Egypt in the fourth century BC, the mercantile counterpart to the nearby town of Canopus

Statue, probably of a Ptolemaic queen, and a completely intact stele bearing a royal decree of 380 BC by which Nectanebo I, first pharaoh of the 30th Dynasty, favours the temple of Neith.

(which was already beginning to develop a reputation for loose living and debauchery that lasted well into the Roman imperial era).

The doomed metropolis

Yet the success of the port city of Thonis was built upon a shaky foundation – literally. The islets upon which the city stood were made of hard clay swept down by the Nile over millennia. As the city prospered, more and larger buildings were constructed, with the weight of hundreds of tonnes of stone compacting the clay even further.

Circumstances were ideal for a process known as silt liquefaction, which occurs when saturated clay is compressed and then shaken violently, as happens in an earthquake. When this takes place the structure of the clay changes from a solid to a fluid – with disastrous consequences for the buildings sitting on top.

It seemed almost as though the gods were conspiring against the people of Thonis. As well as the abrupt and terrifying disappearance of several islets owing to an earthquake, rebuilding was made more difficult by the economic slump following Alexander the Great's conquest of Egypt in 332 BC. After his construction of Alexandria, the new Egyptian cosmopolis immediately started drawing Mediterranean trade away from Thonis.

Meanwhile, changing sea levels along the Egyptian coastline were dramatically affecting cities of the Nile delta. The port of Pelusium up the coast was becoming cut off from the sea, with a marsh developing where the harbour had once been. Thonis had the opposite problem, with rising sea levels slowly overwhelming those islets which had withstood the seismic shock – especially as overbuilding on the remaining islets had caused subsidence that slowly forced the land below sea level. In the eighth century AD a final earthquake completely submerged the once bustling city of Thonis, leaving it some 10 metres (33 feet) under the waters of Aboukir Bay.

Rediscovery

For centuries Thonis and Herakleion were considered separate, but equally mythical cities. Their rediscovery had to wait until the twenty-first century, when marine archaeologists finally had the tools to explore the sunken cities in Aboukir Bay. The exploration by the European Institute for Underwater Archaeology (IEASM), directed by Franck Goddio, began in the 1990s. Their specially developed tools (a nuclear magnetic resonance magnetometer, multi-beam bathymetry, side-scan sonar, sub-bottom profiler and satellite positioning system) finally led to the discovery of Thonis/Herakleion in 2000. The site is about twice the size of Pompeii and completely exploring it will take well over a century.

Thonis Today

The results of the IEASM's underwater investigations have been nothing less than spectacular. For a start, Herodotus was proven right about the existence of Thonis, which was quickly discovered to be Herakleion under a different name. The statues, temples and inscriptions which have been discovered so far have already dramatically altered the historical view of Greco-Egyptian relations. Even though less than 5 per cent of the site has been explored, Thonis has produced a wealth of statues, hieroglyphic inscriptions, coins and jewelry as well as more mundane artefacts that reveal much detail about everyday life in contemporary Egypt.

Perhaps most surprising of all was the discovery in 2010 of the remains of a *baris* river boat built of acacia-thorn planks. The wreckage, found beneath a submerged wharf in Thonis, sent ripples of surprise around the world of marine archaeology. The design and construction of the ship were exactly as Herodotus had described – so now both his mythical city and imaginary river boat have been indisputably transferred into the world of cold, hard fact. Somewhere in the shadows of the Underworld, the old historian must be chuckling.

c. 1650–468 BC
Mycenae
Legendary Beginnings
and a Mysterious End

Here I have seen the face of Agamemnon.

Heinrich Schliemann

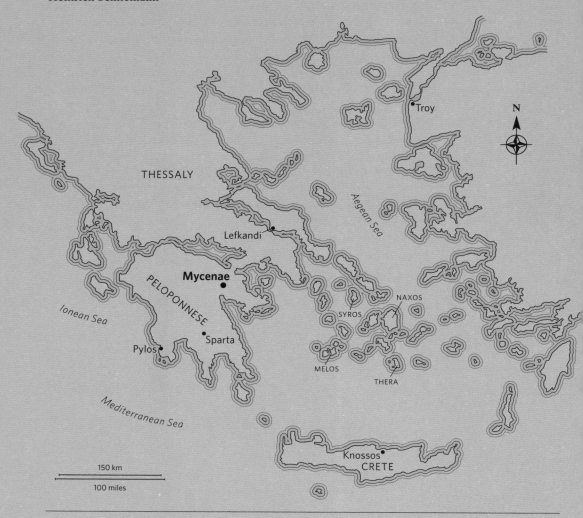

THESSALY

Troy

Aegean Sea

Lefkandi

Mycenae

PELOPONNESE

NAXOS

Ionean Sea

SYROS

Sparta

Pylos

MELOS

THERA

Mediterranean Sea

150 km

100 miles

Knossos
CRETE

N

Seeking the city of Mycenae, one ancient traveller based his search on the town of Nemea, near the gorge where Hercules slew the legendary Nemean Lion. He reasoned that since Eurystheus, the king who gave Hercules this task, was the king of Mycenae, his city must be nearby.

Indeed, there it was, on the left-hand side of the road to Argos, a set of forlorn ruins atop a hill some 200 metres (656 feet) above the surrounding Argolid plain. In his account – the first description of a visit to the ruins of Mycenae – Pausanias, the traveller in question, relates how he wandered through the tumbled walls and found the Lion Gate (*Guide to Greece* 2.15.2–2.18.3). This gate is today considered the most evocative remnant of the ruined city and the civilization that was built around it. Centuries ago, it was equally evocative for Pausanias, that first explorer, who added the site to his handbook for Roman tourists, written around AD 160.

Until then, the ruins of Mycenae had been in a limbo somewhere between lost and forgotten. Dignitaries such as Alexander the Great and the Roman emperor Nero passed by the site, and indeed probably travelled the same road that Pausanias describes. Had they known it was nearby, both men certainly would have wanted to visit the home of Agamemnon, conqueror of Troy, but there is no record that they did so. There were ruins visible on the hilltop, without question, but even in those days Greece had no shortage of ruins. Until Pausanias identified the place,

The so-called Face of Agamemnon is in fact a sixteenth-century BC gold funerary mask of an unknown person, excavated from Grave Circle A in Mycenae.

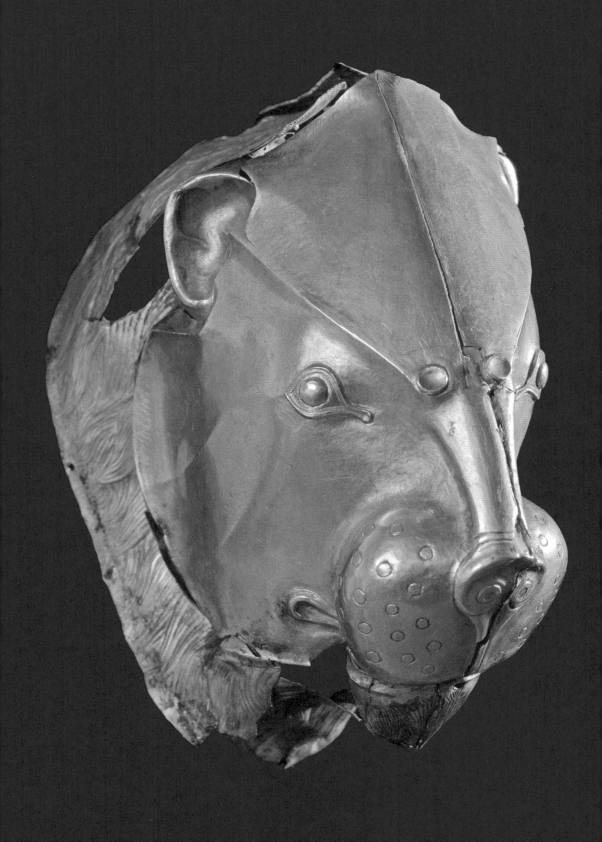

it seems that the remains of legendary Mycenae mouldered in obscurity, known only to local shepherds and the ghosts of those who had known the city in its greatness.

'Great' Mycenae once had been. In his *Iliad*, the poet Homer called it 'Golden Mycenae' and praised the wide streets of this 'well-founded' citadel. At the time Homer describes, Mycenae was a city of some thirty thousand people and traded with Anatolia, the Caucasus, Egypt and Syria. Not only did Mycenaean merchant ships ply the waters of the Aegean Sea, but their warships carried the heroes who besieged Troy. Those same ships were also feared pirate vessels, which dominated the isles of the Cyclades. There are hints that the warriors on these ships also fought as mercenaries in the many wars of the later Bronze Age.

So dominant was Mycenae in the period 1650–1050 BC that this is now known as the Mycenaean era of Greece. However, even though the city came to dominate the northern Peloponnese, Attica (120 kilometres [75 miles] to the northeast) and even Knossos on the island of Crete, Mycenae was never the centre of an empire, or even an extensive kingdom. The geography of Greece was too broken by mountains for the poor communications and weak administrative systems of the day to permit centralized rule over a wide area. Instead, Mycenae as a city was the first among equals – a hegemonic power that so dominated the other citadel-based kingdoms of Greece that many of them were reduced to the status of vassals.

Long after the city had fallen from power, the legend of Mycenae endured. The founder, it was claimed, was none other than the mythical hero Perseus, who still looks down from the constellation bearing his name. One story goes that the hero stopped at a spring and broke off the head of a large mushroom to serve as a cup. While sipping the cool water, Perseus looked over the fertile Argolid plain and realized that this was an excellent site for a city. The spring is now called the Perseia, and the city itself supposedly takes its name from that mushroom – μύκης, or *mycos* in Greek.

Modern archaeologists point out that if the story were true, the legend of Perseus would be improbably old. The site of Mycenae was settled at least eight thousand years ago by a Neolithic people who left behind few traces of their occupation apart from their distinctive 'Rainbow' Ware pottery (actually only black and red). The rest of their archaeological heritage was wiped away by the ambitious building projects of later kings.

Some time around 1350 BC the citadel was built, with walls so massive that later generations called them 'cyclopean', for they believed that only the gigantic craftsman race of the one-eyed

Cyclopes could have constructed them. Some of the lintels and gate jambs are built with blocks of stone weighing over 20 tonnes. A later extension was built to the northeast to secure the spring, which, along with an impressive underground cistern and granaries, meant that Mycenae could withstand siege almost indefinitely. Other structures, such as dams and channels, indicate careful management of the citadel's water supply.

We know many of the rulers of Mycenae from legend. The descendants of the hero Perseus formed the Perseid dynasty, which died out with Eurystheus and Hercules. The Atreid dynasty replaced them. The doings of the cursed members of the House of Atreus would fill a book in their own right, but here it should simply be noted that one of the most impressive remaining structures in Mycenae is allegedly the tomb of one of their last kings – Agamemnon, the Greek leader in Homer's *Iliad*.

This, sometimes known today as the 'Treasury of Atreus', is a beehive-shaped, 'tholos'-style tomb atop the Panagitsa Hill and is impressive even by Mycenaean standards – the stone lintel above the entrance alone weighs 109 tonnes. The king's hall, called the Megaron, also remains impressive even in its dilapidated state. Once, colourful mosaics decorated the floor and vivid frescoes brightened the plastered walls. Among the decorations found at the site is a scarab, gifted around 1360 BC by Amenhotep III of Egypt, who knew the city by its Egyptian name of 'Mwkanu'.

A decorated glass pendant from Mycenae. It is not known if the pattern had any significance or was purely decorative.

We know much less about the common people of Mycenae, for the site was partly reoccupied in the Hellenistic era and those settlers inconsiderately destroyed many traces of the houses from when the city was in its prime. Some houses remain, especially those of palace retainers, which clustered densely around the throne room, and today bear names such as 'the House of Shields', 'the House of the Oil Merchant' and 'the House of the Sphinxes'. From these structures it is clear that Mycenae contained both a sophisticated bureaucracy and abundant merchants and craftsmen. Mycenaean products are regularly unearthed in Egypt, Syria and the Levant.

How the Mycenaeans worshipped their gods is uncertain. Familiar names appear in fragments of Linear B, the script used in Greece at this time, but sometimes the context is unfamiliar – Poseidon appears as a horse god, and Dionysus a fertility god. Athena (Menvra) was the protector of the *wanax*, as the king was called.

Perhaps it was a curse of the gods which destroyed Mycenae in a conflagration which took down not just the city, but the whole Mycenaean civilization. Even now the causes of this 'Bronze Age

collapse' are uncertain, but the archaeological evidence speaks of a catastrophe that severely damaged the city. Repairs were made, and broken walls crudely patched up before the city was destroyed in a further assault. Burned grain and vegetables in the granaries show that the city still had the resources to withstand siege, but evidently the manpower was lacking. Who attacked Mycenae, and why the city was destroyed, are just two of the mysteries surrounding the end of Mycenaean Greece.

When Greece slowly emerged from the subsequent dark age an attempt was made to re-found Mycenae. But the city never reclaimed its lost glory. Power had shifted to different centres, and around 468 BC the hoplites of Argos devastated the re-established Mycenae and expelled the population. Thereafter, all that remained were ruins and a history that was quickly fading into myth.

Mycenae Today

Mycenae was rediscovered in the eighteenth century by one Francesco Vandeyk, who used the two-thousand-year-old *Guide to Greece* to find the location (which would surely have made Pausanias very proud). However, excavations did not begin until over a century later, when a number of archaeologists essayed digs at the site.

Among these was Heinrich Schliemann, the man who rediscovered Troy. He had enthusiastically dug up much of the citadel before the authorities discovered his unauthorized activities and closed him down. Perhaps the most significant of Schliemann's discoveries was a magnificent funeral mask, which he promptly christened 'the Face of Agamemnon'. This mask was beaten from a single sheet of gold, and in fact the abundance of gold found among burial goods at the site shows that Homer was justified in calling the city 'golden'.

The site has been excavated regularly in subsequent years, and a recent geographical survey of the area has led to the discovery of the lower town. This is still being explored and may yet give us considerable detail about the lives of ordinary Mycenaeans.

Mycenae is now a UNESCO World Heritage Site. A museum tells the history of the city and showcases some of the most interesting artefacts. The still largely intact Treasury and tombs, along with the restored and iconic Lion Gate, attract many tourists. Today visitors still proceed through that gate towards the Megaron as visitors did three and a half thousand years ago, though the site is open only from dawn to dusk and there is a small fee to enter.

Gold pins such as this one from Mycenae have been found in Bronze Age sites across the Mediterranean world. It has been suggested that the hole at the back of the 5.9-centimetre (2-inch) long pin allowed it to function as a needle.

307 BC–AD 164
Seleucia-on-the-Tigris
The Vampire City

*The city, through which trade flowed from the Middle East
and China, became one of the greatest in the world.*

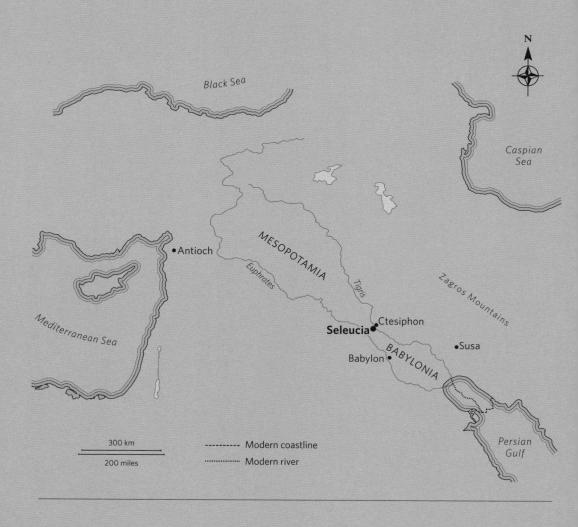

N

Black Sea

Caspian
Sea

MESOPOTAMIA

•Antioch

Euphrates

Tigris

Zagros Mountains

Mediterranean Sea

Ctesiphon

Seleucia•

•Susa

BABYLONIA

Babylon •

Persian
Gulf

300 km

200 miles

- - - - - - - - Modern coastline

· · · · · · · · · Modern river

Even in 311 BC, Babylon was thousands of years old. In its prime the city had been a rival to the Assyrian empire and, even after the Assyrian conquest, remained that empire's most rebellious possession. Proud of their city's ancient heritage, the Babylonians were also prepared to stand up to their latest foreign master, the Macedonian general Seleucus I, who (after some adventures) became ruler of Babylon and Mesopotamia after it had been taken from the Persian empire by Alexander the Great.

Seleucus was a thoughtful sort of general (as one had to be, to survive the vicious infighting that followed the death of Alexander) and he was well aware of the trouble that Babylon had caused the Assyrians. He knew that simply levelling the city would be ineffective – that had been tried before, and every time Babylon had returned, phoenix-like, from the ashes.

Importing a population

Instead, Seleucus decided to bleed away Babylon's lifeblood – the trade and agricultural wealth that had sustained the city through the millennia. He did this by building a new city close by, but at an even more advantageous location, around 35 kilometres (22 miles)

Seleucus I, r. 305–281 BC, a relatively minor general of Alexander the Great who later managed by cunning, diplomacy and military skill to become master of one of the largest empires in the ancient world.

southeast of modern Baghdad. The city was called Seleucia after himself, and when it has to be distinguished from other cities of the same name (Seleucus founded several) the city is called Seleucia-on-the-Tigris. While on the Tigris, the city enjoyed the further advantage of being linked to the Euphrates by the Persian Royal Canal. There was already a city called Opis close by, but this was rapidly absorbed by the new monster metropolis, which Seleucus intended to be the Mesopotamian capital of his massive empire.

Work started between 309 and 301 BC. The historian Appian in his *Syrian Wars* (12.58) gives the interesting detail that the Babylonian astrologer-priests deliberately hid the most auspicious hour for work to begin, but the soldiers of Seleucus spontaneously started work at the correct time anyway. The new city was laid out along Greek lines by architects working to a master plan, so that the main street of the city, a double boulevard, ran arrow-straight from end to end. There was a separate palace and administrative area, and the houses were laid out in neat rectilinear blocks. (Not that the builders were above recycling used materials – one of the bricks used for the city walls bears a stamp dating it to five hundred years before.)

Coin with the head of the Sasanian king Shapur I, r. c. AD 240–70, found at Seleucia-on-the-Tigris. The obverse of the coin shows a fire altar, as the Sasanians considered fire to be sacred.

Seleucus was prepared to let Babylon wither away naturally, so he left the city walls standing (Pausanias, *Guide to Greece* 1.16.3), but he either encouraged or forced much of the population to move to Seleucia, intending to leave Babylon depopulated apart from its priests and temple workers. Exiles from Babylon now shared Seleucia with a population of Macedonians and a substantial number of Jews. The only irregular feature of the neatly laid out new city was the walls that enclosed its 550 hectares (1,360 acres). The outline of these was determined by the river, canal and local topography, and the Roman writer Pliny the Elder describes the city's shape as resembling 'an eagle spreading its wings' (*Natural History* 6.122).

Between east and west

Over the next century the city became one of the greatest in the world, a rival to Alexandria in Egypt and larger than the Seleucid empire's western capital of Antioch. Like Babylon before it, Seleucia was the nexus through which trade flowed between Central Asia, Mesopotamia, India, Africa and Europe. Later, this trade network would expand to include China and points east along that many-branched highway we now call the Silk Road.

The city itself was something of a melting pot. Its pottery shows a fascinating blend of Greek and local styles, and the decorative plaster used on a variety of buildings contains both Greek and

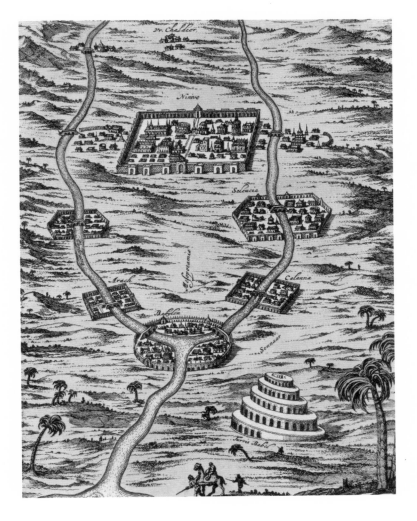

An engraving showing Mesopotamia in Athanasius Kircher's *The Tower of Babel*, published in 1679. Though mostly centred on the biblical story, this map shows what was known of Mesopotamia in the seventeenth century.

Middle Eastern motifs. The local Mesopotamian influence was certainly present in the mix, for at least some people continued the ancient tradition of burying their dead within the structure of their homes.

A new rival

Seleucia continued to serve as an interface between eastern and western culture even as the empire of the Seleucids crumbled and the city fell under Parthian domination in 141 BC. Rather like the Babylonians before them, the Macedonian population of Seleucia bridled at foreign rule, so just like Seleucus, the Parthian kings tried

Detail from the Arch of
Severus in Rome, which
depicts the capture
of Seleucia-on-the-
Tigris by the Romans
in AD 195. Soldiers
from this campaign
are believed to have
brought back plague,
which devastated the
Roman empire.

to weaken the centre of native resistance by building a rival city.
This was Ctesiphon, which became the Parthian capital. For good
measure, the Parthians also founded Vologesocerta as a rival port.

This tactic appears to have been effective, but very slow.
The pottery of Seleucia reflects a decline in standards, and there
are signs of increasing ethnic tensions, which at one point erupted
into a pogrom against the city's Jewish population. According to
the Jewish historian Josephus (*Jewish Antiquities* 18.3.9) some fifty
thousand were killed and the rest fled to Ctesiphon and beyond.

In the end it was not Parthia's rulers who struck the death-blow
to Seleucia, but the Romans. At the start of the second century AD,
Rome was at the height of its power, and the emperor Trajan pushed

Rome's frontiers east to create the new – but short-lived – province of Mesopotamia. In AD 116 Ctesiphon and Seleucia were captured and pillaged.

Yet the city hung on, and was said to still contain 300,000 citizens in AD 165, when the Romans returned. This time, they destroyed Seleucia completely. There is a certain irony in the fact that Avidius Cassius, the Roman commander, claimed as an ancestor Seleucus, who had originally founded the city over three centuries before. This time there was no coming back for Seleucia. When the Romans launched their next assault on Mesopotamia in AD 197, they found nothing but ruins where proud Seleucia had once stood.

Seleucia Today

Part of the buried remains of Seleucia formed a mound known locally as Tell Umar. By the start of the twentieth century the location of the city had been forgotten, not least because the Tigris had changed its course, and the tell now lay 2 kilometres (about a mile) away from the river.

In 1927 Western archaeologists began to excavate the site, believing it to be the city of Opis. Excavations continued sporadically for the next decade, and the ruins were positively identified as the lost city of Seleucia, partly on the strength of the discovery of an elaborate edifice dedicated to Seleucus as the city's founder. Thousands of artefacts have been retrieved, some Greek, some Middle Eastern and others a mixture of both – further proof of the city's role as a cultural mediator between Parthia and the Mediterranean world. These artefacts have allowed historians a reasonably clear picture of how the city functioned, though sadly there is no equivalent of the cuneiform archives that provide so much detail of the urban life of Mesopotamian peoples even more distant in time.

So long as the situation in Iraq deters tourism, those wanting to visit a smaller Seleucia can travel to Turkey to Seleucia Pieria ('Seleucia-by-the-sea'). This was also founded by Seleucus, and has the additional advantage of a nearby beach at the modern seaside town of Çevlik.

720 BC–*c.* AD 700
Sybaris
The Dragon City

The Sybarites developed a fondness for lavish religious festivals, communal feasts and private parties.

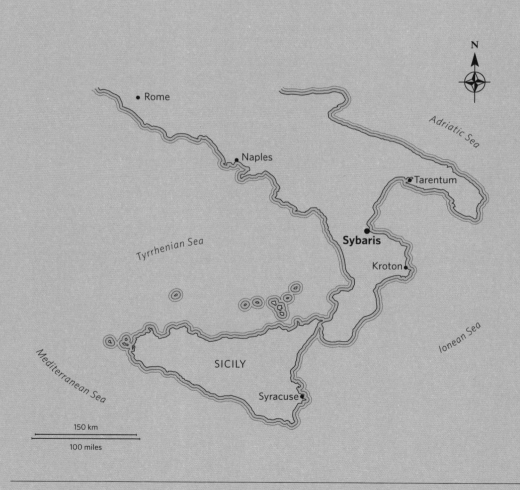

N

Adriatic Sea

Rome

Naples

Tarentum

Tyrrhenian Sea

Sybaris

Kroton

Ionean Sea

SICILY

Mediterranean Sea

Syracuse

150 km

100 miles

The original Sybaris was a monster – a dragon with an insatiable appetite that lived in a cave near the Oracle of Delphi and emerged to snatch livestock and people. However, as generally happened to monsters in Greek myth, Sybaris eventually ran into a hero. This was Eurybarus, and he hauled Sybaris from her den and threw her down the mountainside. The dragon struck her head upon a rock and was killed, but the impact opened up a spring and this source of fresh water was named Sybaris in her memory.

In later years, Greek explorers of the coast of Italy located a fertile plain on the shores of the Gulf of Tarentum. This plain lay between two rivers, one of which they named the Crathis, and the other the Sybaris. It is probable that the Sybaris was so named for the same reason that there is a River Thames in Connecticut – people in an unfamiliar landscape name geographical features that remind them of home.

The swastika had a long history before it was hijacked by the Nazis in the twentieth century. It was used by the Boy Scouts until 1935, as a religious symbol in India, and as a motif on floors in Sybaris in the sixth century BC.

Silver stater from Sybaris, c. 520 BC. Although less than 3 centimetres (1 inch) across, such a coin represented about three days' wages for a skilled worker.

The location was ideal for settlement, and around 720 BC a wave of Greek colonists arrived. Displacing the original inhabitants, who had already built a necropolis and a religious sanctuary on the site, the colonists built their city upon a low ridge near the coast and began to cultivate the rich soil between the rivers. According to legend, the founder of the city was one Sagaris of Helike – a detail that boded ill for the future. (In later years Helike would be struck by an earthquake and then submerged by a tsunami that wiped out the inhabitants. Nor are the jealous gods done with Helike – recently discovered and excavated, it is now one of the most endangered archaeological sites in the world, thanks to climate change.)

Sybaris was not the first Greek city to be founded in southern Italy. In fact, so abundant were Greek colonies in the region that later ages have come to refer to it as Magna Graecia – 'Greater Greece'. Many of its cities were larger and more powerful than those in Greece itself. Indeed, such Greek settlements as Tarentum, Naples and Syracuse remain major urban centres today. At around the time when Sybaris was founded, another colony sprang up somewhat further down the coast – the city of Kroton.

One of the major factors that prevented the Greeks from developing an empire in the manner of the Assyrians and Romans was that while they were prepared to battle native tribes and the Phoenicians, with whom they were bitter trading rivals, they reserved their most venomous hatred for the inhabitants of other Greek cities. So it was with Kroton and Sybaris.

It did not help that the two cities developed completely different approaches to life. Fuelled by the agricultural wealth of its fertile fields, Sybaris prospered, becoming one of the most powerful cities of Magna Graecia. The Greek historian Diodorus (*History* 12.9) puts its population at 300,000 around 510 BC, which makes Sybaris almost exactly the same size as Athens at the time. The Sybarites developed a fondness for lavish religious festivals, communal feasts and private parties. So extensive was this love of the good life that the city has given the modern world the adjective 'sybaritic' for anything luxurious, bordering upon decadence.

This happy hedonism was regarded with disdain by the people of Kroton, who opted for a lifestyle closer to the Spartan approach, though with greater regard for the liberal arts. In fact, the philosopher and mathematician Pythagoras originally set up shop in Kroton, which was also famed for the quality of its doctors.

Unlike the somewhat insular Krotonites (who eventually found Pythagoras's ideas too challenging and expelled him) the Sybarites welcomed immigrants. In fact, they granted citizenship to so many that there was a backlash, leading to *stasis* – the internal strife which was the ruin of many a Greek city in the Classical era. Eventually a large bloc of the immigrant population was forced to flee for their lives, and took refuge in Kroton. The Sybarites immediately sent ambassadors to Kroton demanding that the refugees be handed over – or else.

According to Diodorus, the people of Kroton were reluctant to antagonize their more powerful neighbour, and were inclined to hand over the supplicants. But Pythagoras addressed the assembly and convinced its members to reject the Sybarite demands, even if this meant war.

Modern historians feel that, while this incident may have sparked conflict, it is probable that trouble had already been brewing. The two cities were close neighbours and keen competitors for trade between the Italian interior and other Mediterranean cultures. Given the fondness of Greek cities for settling their differences on the battlefield, eventual conflict was inevitable.

No account of the war survives, but the result is well known. Despite their superior numbers the Sybarites were utterly defeated. 'In their fury the Krotonites took no-one prisoner but slew everyone who fell into their hands. The majority of the people of Sybaris perished in this manner, and thereafter they [the hoplites of Kroton] fell upon the city of Sybaris and destroyed it utterly' (Diodorus, *History* 12.10). According to some reports the people of Kroton felt so strongly about their neighbours that they diverted the Crathis river to flow over the demolished city, though modern research suggests that this would have been impracticable.

A terracotta arula (small altar) from Sybaris showing lions killing a pig, sixth century BC.

The amphitheatre at
Sybaris. According
to one ancient writer
(Aelian, *De Natura
Animalium* 16), Sybarite
horses were trained
to dance at such
venues. Sadly, when
the Sybarite cavalry
attempted to charge
the enemy, the
Krotonites responded
by playing music and
counter-attacked the
dancing horses and
their confused riders.

For half a century Sybaris lay desolate, but the site was too
attractive to remain abandoned. New settlers arrived from Thessaly,
only to receive a less-than-warm welcome from Kroton, whose
people liked the ruins of Sybaris just as they were. The new
population of Sybaris appealed for help from the Athenians,
whose power was growing to create a handy little empire of island
states. The Athenians of that period were inventive, dynamic and
ambitious, but sometimes behaved regrettably. They did not so
much help the Sybarites as kick them out of their own city, which
in 444 BC the Athenians renamed Thurii.

The displaced Sybarites skulked further south, where they
founded a new city on the banks of the Traeis river. This fourth
attempt to found Sybaris was short-lived, for some time after
350 BC the city was destroyed by the Brutti, a native Italian people.

Thurii remained a site of some importance right through the
Roman era. In fact the emperor Augustus originally bore the name
'Thurinus' because his father had won a minor victory nearby.
However, during the medieval period the river delta shifted and
mudbanks eventually blocked the city from the sea. Thurii was
abandoned, and eventually buried under silt from the rivers as
the dragon Sybaris finally took her revenge.

Sybaris Today

Sybaris is still a lost city, in that archaeologists are not certain whether they have found it. The best bet is a set of ruins beside the Roman remains of the city of Thurii, near the modern town of Sibari (whose inhabitants are not noticeably decadent). The ruins were discovered in 1968 amid some fanfare, but definite proof of identity is still not forthcoming.

Kroton has survived through the ages and is currently the modern metropolis of Crotone in Calabria.

The presumed site of Sybaris is presently an active archaeological dig, where work has progressed slowly through layers dating to Late Antiquity and the Roman era. The period of Greek exploration was only beginning to be investigated in 2022, and so far a theatre and the remains of a colonnaded street have come to light. Many of the discoveries taken from the site are stored at the nearby National Archaeological Museum of Sibaritide. Both the museum and the excavations are open to tourists.

c. 1250 BC–*c.* AD 1400
Plataea
The Little City That Could

The site of the epic battle that freed
Greece from Persian domination.

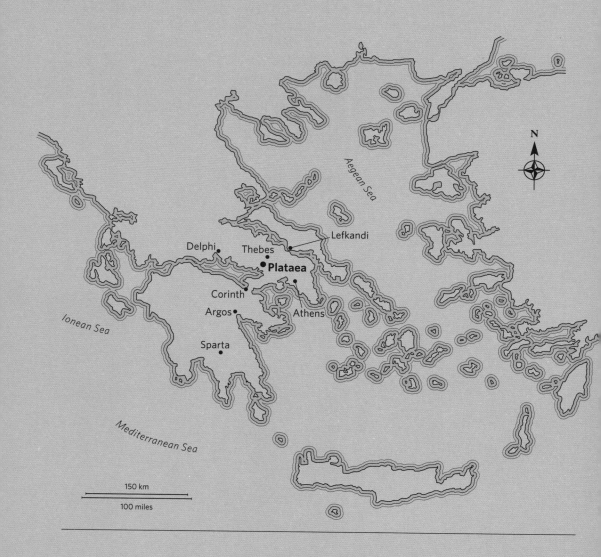

Aegean Sea

N

Lefkandi

Delphi Thebes
 Plataea

Corinth

Argos

Athens

Ionean Sea

Sparta

Mediterranean Sea

150 km

100 miles

For a small mountain city, Plataea looms large in the history of ancient Greece. The city in many ways epitomizes the Greek character in those days. The citizens were energetic, heroic and inventive, yet unable to prevent their city being destroyed – repeatedly – by their nation's dysfunctional politics. Each time Plataea was levelled, its stubborn inhabitants rebuilt it.

Even in ancient times there was considerable debate as to who founded Plataea and when. The nearby Thebans claimed that they founded the little city, which was situated on a large flat area on the slopes of Mount Cithaeron overlooking the Boeotian plain. The Plataeans themselves indignantly denied that their ancestors were Theban colonists, and claimed descent from their namesake Plataea, a water nymph and the daughter of Asopus, the god of the nearby river.

Modern archaeologists have dug into the debate (literally) and tentatively come down on the side of the Thebans. There are no signs that Plataea was occupied before the 'palace period' of the Mycenaean era (1400–1200 BC), and the Thebans of that time would have had good reason to occupy the site. The fortress that later became Plataea was within 10 kilometres (6 miles) of Thebes and occupied a strategic point on the vital road to Corinth.

The Classical city of Plataea as imagined in the eighteenth century in this woodcut from Chevalier de Folard's *Histoire de Polybe*.

Aristides, who commanded
the Athenian troops at the
Battle of Plataea, sacrifices
to honour the spirits of dead
Plataean warriors.

Against Thebes and Persia

Plataea first enters the historical record around half a millennium after its foundation, having spent most of the intervening period as a fortress of last resort for the farmers who cultivated the rich plains around the River Asopus. As Greek civilization regained strength following the Bronze Age collapse, the Thebans attempted to restore their hegemony over the Plataeans. Plataea appealed to the Spartans, who were the greatest military power in Greece at that time, for help.

However, the Spartans were famously reluctant to deploy their army outside the Peloponnese and suggested that the Plataeans turn to the Athenians instead. The historian Herodotus (who was no admirer of Sparta) alleges that the Spartans wished to stir up trouble between Athens and Thebes – which their suggestion did. When the Thebans tried to force Plataea into their confederacy, they were met by an Athenian army which gave them a sound beating. Thereafter, the River Asopus became the boundary between Thebes and Plataea and the Plataeans became eternally grateful to the Athenians.

In 490 BC, Athens stood alone against the might of the Persian army on the plain of Marathon, northeast of Athens. The Spartans, to their later embarrassment, had declined to help the Athenians, who were therefore deeply concerned to observe another force marching to the battlefield. Since no-one was helping the Athenians, they assumed the new arrivals must be enemies. Instead, it turned out that the newcomers were friendly reinforcements from Plataea and this contingent, though small, consisted of every able-bodied Plataean male who could be crammed into a set of armour.

After the Persian defeat the Athenians remembered Plataea's help with gratitude, and the Persians with vindictive resentment. When the Persians returned to Greece a decade later, their new and improved invasion force defeated the Spartans at Thermopylae and then went on to flatten both Athens and Plataea. In 479 BC the Persian Wars reached a climax when a combined Greek army defeated the Persians (and Thebans) in a pitched battle outside the ruins of Plataea, and the Persians were finally driven from Greece. Plataea was rebuilt by a grateful nation and its citizens were given extra privileges in Athens.

Against Sparta

Sadly, Greek unity in the face of the Persian threat did not endure. Athens started to oppress its former allies and forced them to become unwilling subjects of its growing empire. This alarmed the Spartans, who joined Corinth in an anti-Athenian alliance. Thebes joined this group, which put Plataea automatically into the Athenian camp.

When hostility evolved into open warfare, the Thebans tried to take Plataea out of the war at once by launching a surprise preemptive strike that captured the city. However, once the Plataeans realized that the Theban advance guard was only a few hundred men, they massacred the invaders and prepared to withstand siege. The strategic location of Plataea meant that the city would severely interfere with attacks on Athens, so the Spartans tried hard to take the place.

Direct assaults on the walls failed. A ramp leading up to the wall failed because the Plataeans tunnelled under their own walls and took earth from beneath the ramp as fast as the Spartans put it on top. A tower built alongside the wall failed because the Plataeans built up their wall faster than the Spartans could enlarge the tower. An ingenious attempt to destroy the gates using a large flame-throwing device failed when a change in the wind nearly incinerated the Spartan camp.

In the end the Spartans settled on the tried-and-trusted technique of sitting outside the walls and waiting for the occupants of the city to starve. The Plataeans staged a breakout that evacuated most of the population, but hunger eventually forced the remaining defenders to surrender in 427 BC. The aggrieved Spartans massacred the garrison and Plataea was demolished once again.

Thebes, again, and an imperial possession

The Thebans built a katagogion (a type of guest house) and a large temple to Hera on the site of Plataea. Once the Peloponnesian War was over (Athens lost) the Plataeans rebuilt their city in the 370s. The Plataeans were adamant that they did not want to join the Theban confederacy, and since the rebuilt city infringed upon the lands now dedicated to Hera, in 373 BC the Thebans used this excuse to flatten Plataea once more.

Fortunately for the Plataeans, Thebes over-reached itself in defying the rising power of Macedonia. After agreeing to work with the Macedonian king Philip II (who spent part of his youth in Thebes), the city rebelled against Philip's son Alexander the Great. Alexander made his feelings plain by removing Thebes from the map and ostentatiously rebuilding Plataea. Alexander was about to launch a war against Persia and wanted to show solidarity with the little city that had stood up to both the might of the Persian empire and Theban bullying.

Plataea thrived under the control of first the Macedonians and later the Romans. As part of a larger empire, Plataea lost its strategic importance, and thus the reason why others kept wanting to demolish it. In fact, Plataea remained a functioning community through the rest of the Roman empire and the Byzantine empire that replaced it. With the fall of the Byzantine empire, Plataea seems finally to have been abandoned.

Plataea Today

Ancient Plataea lies in ruins, and though these remains are not particularly spectacular, they are often visited by tourists with an interest in military history who want to see for themselves the site of the epic battle of Plataea, which freed Greece from Persian domination.

A village called Plataies has sprung up a few kilometres from the original site. After an administrative reform in 2011, this village was brought under the control of the municipality of Thebes. And so, after two and a half thousand years, Thebes has finally managed to achieve its ancient objective of bringing Plataea under its control.

While deadly at a distance, Persian bowmen stood little chance against Greek hoplites at close quarters – as this red-figure vase from the time of the Persian Wars (c. 470 BC) graphically demonstrates.

c. 3000 BC–AD 500
Taxila
A City in Three Instalments

The world's first university, teaching topics such as medicine, military science and law.

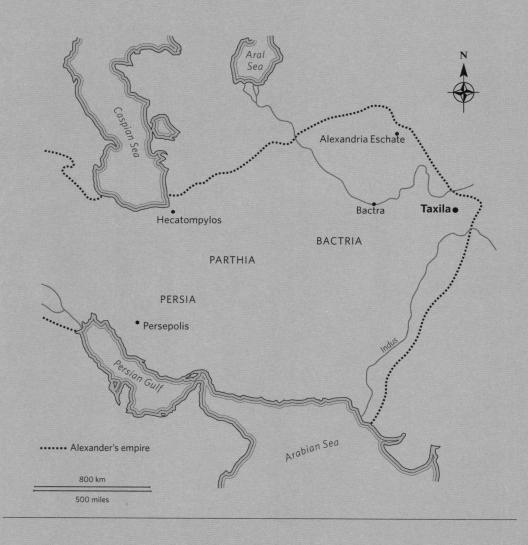

Alexander's empire

800 km

500 miles

The city of Taxila stood for around 1,500 years on a hill overlooking the River Tamra Nala, some 32 kilometres (20 miles) northwest of Pakistan's modern capital, Islamabad. The location put Taxila at a nexus where the different civilizations of Eurasia met, traded and fought. Taxila was visited by the Greek philosopher Apollonius of Tyana in the first century AD and by the Chinese monk Xuanzang in the seventh. Among those who at various times walked the city's streets were Achaemenid Persians, Greek soldiers of the army of Alexander the Great, Indians of the Mauryan empire, Scythians, Parthians, Kushans and Huns.

Origins

This second-century AD relief showing Buddha and monks on the stupa at the Jaulian monastery, Taxila, demonstrates a mix of Indian, Greek and Persian artistic styles.

Early agricultural settlements first sprang up in the area around 3500 BC, at about the time that the first cities were becoming established in Mesopotamia, some 3,000 kilometres (1,865 miles) to the west. The first settlement at Taxila formed at what is today called the Saraikala mound, and has produced artefacts from the Stone Age through to the Bronze Age, with some fascinating tools

Cetus (a sea monster) from Greek myth is seen here in two paterae from Taxila, on the left being ridden by an unknown hero, and on the right by a Neriad (sea nymph) and a cherub.

A gable border with a relief of richly dressed individuals, possibly worshippers.

Man riding the elephant-styled spout of an ewer of the first century AD.

showing the transition between the two eras. Those with a more romantic disposition might prefer to accept the myth that the city was founded by one Taksa, nephew of the Hindu god Rama, who called the city Takshashila after himself.

Certainly the city was always called Taxila, though another etymology suggests that this means 'the city of cut stone'. However, the collapse of the Indus Valley civilization brought this version of Taxila to an end. When the city was re-founded some time around 700 BC it was at a slightly different location, on a site now known as the Bhir mound.

It appears that the people behind the foundation were probably the Achaemenid Persians, who saw the need for a city at this increasingly important trade hub. Archaeology reveals that the city appears to have grown organically from a trading post, to a large emporium (trading centre), to a fully fledged city. One long street – probably the original road along which the first buildings were erected – ran from end to end of this incarnation of Taxila, with later shops and houses built on lanes and alleys that meandered off to either side.

There was, however, a sophisticated water drainage system and soak wells (an early version of the septic tank) for sewage. Unlike many early city-states in the Mediterranean world, Taxila grew up within an organized empire, and there seems to have been no attempt to build defensive walls. The city appears to have moved equably between the control of the Persian empire and the rival Indian powers to the south. In those intervals when no state was strong enough to control it, Taxila continued as an independent city.

Taxila was independent under the rule of one King Omphis (Ambhi) when the army of Alexander the Great came calling around 326 BC. The city put up no resistance and joined the Macedonian empire, with a party atmosphere created by sacrifices, equestrian games and gymnastic events. It helped that Alexander was a great admirer of learning, and Taxila was already famed for its wise men – a reputation which was only to grow in later centuries. The historian Arrian (*Anabasis* 7.1.6) says that Alexander was so impressed by these sages that he attempted to recruit some of them to his royal court.

Alexander's empire was short-lived, and his Seleucid successors more interested in ruling those parts of the empire nearer to Greece and the Mediterranean. By 317 BC the city was under Indian rule again as part of the Maurya empire founded by Chandragupta. Buddhism was gaining traction in India, and Taxila became one of the great centres of learning for that religion. As well as Buddhist

The third-century BC 'Great' or Dharmarajika Stupa at Taxila. The site was devastated by raiders and abandoned in the fifth century AD.

doctrine, students came to Taxila to learn topics such as medicine, military science and law. Some have argued that this makes Taxila the world's first university, though there was no fixed curriculum – teachers set their own standards and syllabus, and there was no graduation. Students tended to start as teenagers and left when their teacher was satisfied that they had learned enough.

Alexander's empire in the east had collapsed, but it left behind a fascinating Indo-Greek state called the Bactrian kingdom. Though separated from the west by the new empire of the Parthians, Bactria was to remain a flourishing state for several centuries to come. When the Bactrians seized control of Taxila the defenceless nature of the site evidently distressed them, for they relocated the city once again to a site across the river which is today called the Sirkap mound. The natural defences of this site were supplemented by massive stone walls running for some 5 kilometres (3 miles) around the city, with large bastions built into them.

A decorative stone bracket from Taxila showing a cherubic young man holding a fly-whisk.

Now with substantial defences, Taxila survived the waxing and waning of Bactrian power by fluctuating between being a Bactrian city and an independent city-state. The coinage minted by independent Taxila shows a fascinating mix of cultural influences, with Greek legends (for example) portrayed in Indian style. The city itself shows clear indications of Greek influence, for this incarnation was laid out according to the town-planning principles of the Greek Hippodamus; but the Buddhist influence remained dominant.

Later Taxila

At the start of the first century BC Taxila acquired a new set of rulers when the last Bactrian king was overthrown by the Indo-Scythians. It may have been around this time that the Roman writer Strabo received reports from the east, and he left this description in his *Geography* (15.1.62):

Some strange and unusual customs at Taxila:

People who cannot afford a dowry for their daughters bring them to the market place when they reach marriageable age and summon a crowd by trumpets ... should any man be interested, they expose her rear and then her front up to the shoulders. If the man is pleased and the woman allows herself to be persuaded, they are married.

The dead are thrown out to be devoured by vultures.

An elaborately carved disc stone from Taxila in the first century BC. Palmettes and lotus buds are woven into an aesthetically pleasing pattern.

Another mention of Taxila in the Western corpus of ancient writing comes from the Roman author Aelian, whose *De Natura Animalium* (12.8) contains the observation that the elephants from this area were larger than average.

The decline of the Roman empire in the west led to the decline of Taxila, too, as the trade along the Silk Road that had enriched it withered. After further vicissitudes, in AD 450 Taxila was invaded by a tribe affiliated with the Hephthalites (White Huns). Subsequent attacks saw the city's Buddhist monasteries and places of learning destroyed, and though the remnants of the city survived within the short-lived Hunnic empire, Taxila was essentially a ghost town. The last recorded visitor in AD 645 (the Chinese monk Xuanzang) reported largely desolate ruins. Thereafter, Taxila was lost to humanity for the next thousand years.

Taxila Today

Now in its fourth incarnation, Taxila is a modern city close enough to the original (which was rediscovered in the 1860s) for the ancient ruins to be endangered by industrial pollution, looting and nearby limestone quarries. A World Heritage Site, Taxila is listed by UNESCO as on the verge of being lost once more due to twenty-first-century damage.

Many of the artefacts from Taxila are now stored in a dedicated museum at the site, which has one of the most significant collections of Greco-Indian Buddhist sculptures in the world.

83 BC–*c.* AD 850
Tigranocerta
Lost Capital of a Lost Empire

*One of the few places where the cultures
of east and west combined peacefully.*

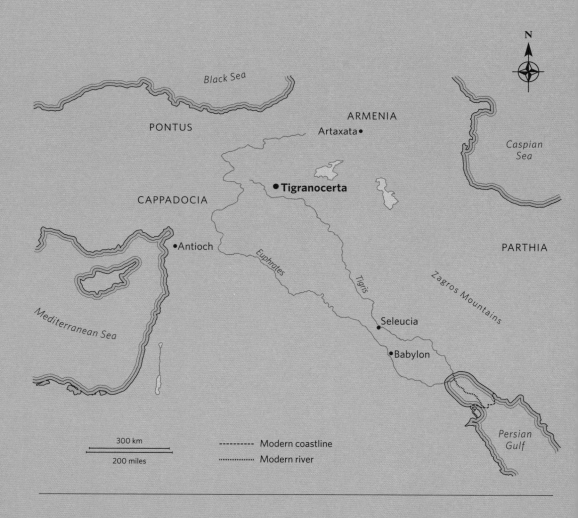

The dream of Alexander the Great was to create a culture in the east that was a fusion of Greek and Persian. This aspiration died along with Alexander himself, for his chauvinistically Macedonian generals saw no need to change what they regarded as a winning formula. Therefore, subsequent settlement in the areas conquered by Alexander saw Greek cities overlaid upon the native culture with little formal mingling between the two. For a glimpse of what might have been had Alexander's aspirations come to fruition, we have to turn to a later king who founded his new capital city upon Alexander's ideal.

The Armenian empire

We may not think of Armenia as an imperial power, yet two thousand years ago the Artaxid empire of Armenia extended from the Caspian Sea to the Mediterranean. The ruler was Tigranes II, whose feats have caused him to be referred to by modern historians – and some ancient Greeks – as 'Tigranes the Great'.

In the first century BC the Levant was undergoing a period of political confusion. The power of the Seleucid empire was fast ebbing (Seleucus was a general of Alexander who had taken control of a

Tigranocerta Artsakh, located in modern-day Azerbaijan, one of a number of cities founded by the Artaxid empire of Armenia and named Tigranocerta. The precise location of the Tigranocerta that served as the capital founded by Tigranes II ('the Great') is unknown.

vast swathe of territory from Bactria to the Mediterranean coast) and the cities of the area were looking for a new protector. During this period of near-anarchy Armenia flourished as a relatively secure haven, offered safety by its natural mountain defences. Tigranes leveraged the natural advantages of his country's position to build a sprawling multi-ethnic empire, which he maintained with a mixture of military force and shrewd politics.

A new capital

Tigranes' new empire needed a new capital city. The previous Armenian capital, Artaxata, was too deep in the Armenian hinterland to be easily accessible to many in his new southern domains of Tigranes. Therefore Tigranes chose a new site, locating this on the famed 'Royal Road' which had once linked the Mediterranean possessions of the Achaemenid Persian empire with its Iranian heartlands.

Like many rulers before and since, Tigranes named his new capital after himself: Tigranocerta, 'the city founded by Tigranes'. Work on the new city began in 83 BC.

As this city was to be his memorial, Tigranes went all out to make it as splendid as the resources of his considerable empire would allow. The king himself was a man of his time, influenced by the multiple poles of Greek, Persian and his native Armenian cultures. Reflecting its monarch, Tigranocerta assumed this same multicultural outlook.

Tetradrachm with Tigranes II on the front, and Tyche (Fortuna) of Antioch on the obverse. Since Antioch was part of the crumbling Seleucid empire, this coin reflects the imperial ambitions of Tigranes.

Where Greece and Persia combined

Tigranocerta included Greek civic amenities from the start. Tigranes was a great admirer of Greek philosophers and playwrights, and constructed a large theatre for his new citizens, probably along with a Greek-style agora and gymnasium. Yet outside the walls he built himself a Persian-style palace complete with hunting grounds and a pleasure garden (called a 'paradise', from the Greek adaptation of the Avestan *pairidaeza* meaning 'enclosure' or 'park').

All the city needed now was a population, and Tigranes had a good idea where he could find one. He leaned towards Hellenistic culture partly because he had a Hellenic wife, called Cleopatra. (Cleopatra was originally a Greek rather than Egyptian name – in Greek myth an early Cleopatra was the daughter of Boreas, the north wind.) The father of Tigranes' Cleopatra was also an ambitious and expansionist monarch, namely Mithridates of Pontus, who was at that time creating a handy kingdom spanning much of Anatolia and the Crimea.

The ambitions of both Mithridates and Tigranes extended towards Cappadocia, a sprawling and disorganized kingdom in the south of Anatolia. Rather than squabble over the spoils, Tigranes and Mithridates appear to have amicably agreed to a settlement – Mithridates would install a puppet king in Cappadocia, and Tigranes would deport some 300,000 Cappadocians to Armenia to form the basis of his new urban population.

Many volunteers joined this conscript population, and the biographer Plutarch reports that civic pride ran high. 'The place was packed with riches, and everybody – whether a prince or a private citizen – competed with the king in beautifying and extending the city' (*Lucullus* 26.2). Hebrews from Palestine, Aramaic peoples from Mesopotamia and Arabs from the south soon contributed to the cosmopolitan life of Tigranocerta.

The Roman catastrophe

The plunder of Cappadocia brought riches but also problems for Tigranes. The kingdom that he and Mithridates had so carelessly despoiled was under the protection of the Roman Republic. And at this time the Roman Republic was militaristic, warlike and led by politicians desperate for glory and cash to support the ever-increasing cost of aristocratic life.

Accordingly, the Romans picked a fight with Mithridates with the aim of looting Pontus. At first this did not go well for them, because Mithridates was no passive victim. He not only threw back the Romans but conquered all of Asia Minor and parts of Greece, killing tens of thousands of Romans in the process. Yet Rome was famously stubborn, and eventually the legions pushed Mithridates out of his kingdom, forcing him to take refuge with his son-in-law in Tigranocerta.

When Tigranes refused to surrender Mithridates to the Romans, the Romans (spurred on by the prospect of plundering the wealth of the Armenian empire) came to get him. The result was a lopsided battle fought between Rome and Armenia in 69 BC just southwest of the still partly unfinished walls of Tigranocerta. Tigranes had up to 100,000 men in his army, while the Roman general Lucullus appears to have had maybe a tenth of that number. Tigranes joked, when looking at the pitiful size of the Roman force, 'If this is a diplomatic mission it is too large, if it is an invasion force, it is much too small.'

Illustration of a battle between Romans and Armenians, from a manuscript compiled in 1475. Although incorrect in almost every detail, this picture gives an interesting insight into how the ancient world was perceived in a later era.

The fall of Tigranocerta

Small the Roman force might be, but it was made up of highly experienced and motivated legionaries keen to get the battle over with so they could finally be discharged and go home. Since the army of Tigranes was too large to take on directly, Lucullus wheeled his men to one flank of his unwieldy enemy and set them to mowing through the ranks of their opponents from there towards the centre.

Most of Tigranes' army had not wanted to be there in the first place, and morale collapsed in the face of the ferocious Roman attack. Tigranes was forced to flee and his city was left exposed to the Romans. The Cappadocian population of Tigranocerta made no secret of which side they were on, and even cheered on Lucullus before the battle. The city walls, even unfinished, were around

20 metres (12½ feet) in height and so thick that they had stables built into them. Yet this counted for nothing, because the inhabitants enthusiastically opened the gates and welcomed in the invaders.

Although Tigranes managed to rescue his harem and much of the royal treasury, the Romans looted an estimated 8,000 talents of gold (a talent being around 25 kilograms [55 pounds]). Lucullus then allowed the captive Cappadocian population to return to their homeland and set the city ablaze before his departure.

Later Tigranocerta

Tigranocerta recovered from the Roman sack, but it never regained its imperial splendour. When the Roman dynast Pompey the Great came to the region a decade later, he re-established Tigranocerta as an administrative centre. The city featured again in the wars between the Parthians and the Romans in the first century AD, because Armenia was caught between those two rival empires and frequently relied upon adroit diplomacy to avoid being crushed by one power or the other. The Romans briefly occupied Tigranocerta once more in AD 83, but did little damage and departed after some successful negotiations.

Tigranocerta remained a prominent regional city thereafter and in the fourth century came under direct Roman control. When the Eastern Roman empire became the Byzantine empire the city was renamed Martyropolis, to celebrate the Christian martyrs. Then in the seventh century the city was renamed again, as Mayarfarkin, after it had fallen to the Arab Umayyad caliphate – but by then it was already in steep decline.

Thereafter the once-proud capital slowly became a deserted ruin, and by the medieval period its whereabouts had been forgotten altogether.

Tigranocerta Today

The precise location of the capital city of Tigranes remains a mystery. It is generally assumed to lie in Diyarbakır province, in the Kurdish region of modern Turkey, on the Tigris or Batman river, probably near the town of Silvan. However, so far Tigranocerta has evaded the efforts of archaeologists to pin down its whereabouts. It remains, therefore, only a symbol of Armenia's brief period as an imperial power, and of one of the few times and places where the cultures of east and west combined peacefully.

c. 510–330 BC
Persepolis
Political Symbol

Persepolis was built as a political symbol,
and its destruction was a symbolic political act.

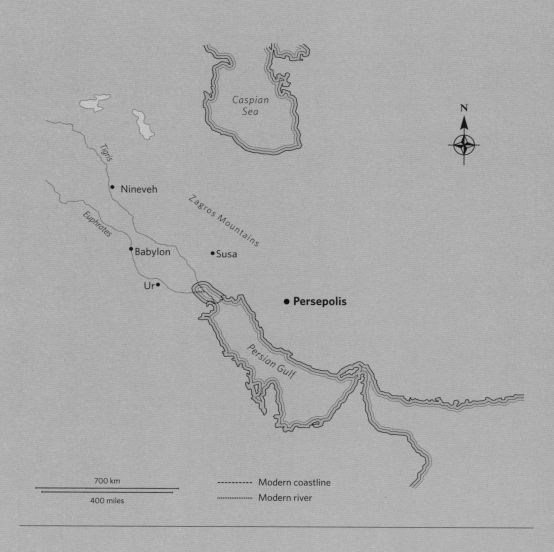

Cities are of many types, and not all are built simply to house people. Persepolis was an extreme example, in that this capital city did not have much of a population at all. In fact, some researchers have speculated that the city was virtually empty for large parts of each year.

Lying at the foot of the 'Mountain of Mercy' (Kuh-e Rahmat), Persepolis was once the imperial heart of the largest empire, by area, in the ancient world. At its height the Achaemenid Persian empire stretched from the shores of the Mediterranean and the southern cataracts of the Nile to the slopes of the Himalayas and the banks of the Indus river.

This was the empire of Cyrus the Great, whose successors threw down the temples on the Acropolis of Athens and slaughtered the Spartans at Thermopylae. The Persian ruler was called the 'King of Kings' and this was no empty title. Literally hundreds of rulers of kingdoms, both great and small, came under his sway, for so vast was the Persian empire that one man could not directly rule it all.

One of the early successors to Cyrus, King Darāyavauš (known by the Greeks as Darius I, 'the Great') realized that Persia's sprawling

Highly stylized, yet still powerfully evocative: the distinctive Persian art of the Achaemenid period. Here we see a lion grapple with its prey while a procession moves up the stairway behind.

This relief from the 'Hall of a Hundred Columns' contains enough detail for the Median nobleman to be identified by his rounded felt cap and distinctive belt. He holds the hand of someone in a Persian robe, signifying the amity between the two peoples.

and cosmopolitan empire needed a capital city that symbolized the unity of government and people. 'Ahuramazda [chief of the Persian gods] decided that this fortress be built, and all the other gods agreed. I built it, and built it secure and functional and beautiful'. So Darius informed posterity in the foundation stone which he laid down, and which was discovered by archaeologists of a later millennium. He called the city 'Parsa', which the Greeks transliterated as 'Persepolis', both names meaning 'City of the Persians'.

Construction began around 510 BC with a massive artificial platform, upon which the principal buildings were to be placed. Made of huge blocks of unmortared stone, this terrace still stands today. It begins at ground level on the east side abutting the mountain and then stretches across the downhill slope, so that the westernmost point is a wall over 12 metres (39 feet) high. The total site covers a vast 125,000 square metres (30 acres) and looks out over the expanse of the Marvdasht plain, a fertile area watered by the confluence of the Pulvar and Kor rivers. (Today this area is best known for the grapes grown around the regional centre of Shiraz, which produce a wine remarked upon favourably by Marco Polo and many later travellers.)

Darius not only created Persepolis but also rebuilt the cities of Ecbatana and Susa as regional capitals, for despite its great significance as the ceremonial centre of the empire, Persepolis was not ideally suited as an administrative centre. It lies in somewhat inaccessible terrain some 850 kilometres (530 miles) south of Tehran, in present-day Iran, and travel there would have been very difficult in the winter months.

By the time that Darius died his city was a stunning monument, but incomplete. His successors were still adding to it almost two centuries later, by which time Persepolis had become the summer residence of the King of Kings, and the place where lesser kings came to pledge allegiance to their sovereign. We know this because bas-reliefs on the still-standing walls depict twenty-three of the subject peoples arriving to pay homage. So exact are these depictions that most of the nationalities can be identified. The ambassadors bear gifts of gold and silver vases, jewels and exotic animals, rare spices and finely woven fabrics, while royal guards and Persian nobles look on.

Such occasions were at their most spectacular over the vernal equinox, which marked the Persian new year (and is still a festival in present-day Iran). Those coming to pledge allegiance approached through the main gate, where the monumental Persepolitan stairway was cut into the western wall, wide enough that the king could come and go on horseback without the royal feet touching the ground. After ascending this staircase, delegates would gather in a small courtyard and await access, through what is today called the Gate of All Nations, to the towering doors of the Apadana, or audience hall, a building so large it could hold thousands of people.

The Apadana was the biggest and most grandiose of the buildings of Persepolis, deliberately designed by Darius to overawe visitors. Darius never lived to see the finished version, but he would have been impressed by the structure completed by his successor Xerxes. The walls were inlaid with marble, but were mainly of native grey limestone polished to a mirror finish. Even today the remains of the Apadana are impressive, though only thirteen huge columns remain standing.

These columns are remarkably tall and slender, of a type unique to the Persian empire. They differ from the Greek style in that the round, lightly fluted shafts still show features of the original wooden type (which was made from the tall cedars of the Lebanon), and the capitals supporting the roof take the form of two animals back-to-back. This design allows the roof beams to rest directly on the animals' heads, for extra support. The result is a distinctively Persian style created by a fusion of Greek, Egyptian and Babylonian elements – a fitting reflection of Persia's far-flung and multicultural empire.

As time went on, each of the Persian kings added new structures to the terrace. Some were splendid palaces, and others residential quarters for the king and his courtiers. More modest residences have been discovered off the main terrace, and it is speculated that these housed the host of artisans who lived permanently at

'Render unto Caesar ...' Representatives from subject nations ascend the Great Stairway in Persepolis to give tribute as tokens of submission to the Persian king.

Previous pages
The ruins of Persepolis
with the view across the
valley. The mountains
in the background had
to be crossed in order to
approach the royal city.

the site, dedicating their careers to the ongoing building project that was Persepolis.

As well as artisans, other semi-permanent residents were the administrators who had the job of keeping the city running. While much of the administration of the empire was done in the regional capitals, the clerks of Persepolis kept careful track of the goods supplied by farmers and who still owed supplies of wheat, wine or livestock. Other records noted the whereabouts and logistical capabilities of villages, fortresses, towns and royal estates in the Persepolis administrative area.

Persepolis was built as a political symbol, and its destruction was a symbolic political act. The destroyer was Alexander the Great, who captured the city in 331 BC. The city's inaccessibility worked to its advantage, and the army of Alexander had a hard time getting through the mountains and their stubborn Persian defenders.

Alexander was eager to gain control of Persepolis, and not just for the booty stored in the royal treasuries. In becoming master of the Persian capital city, Alexander could consolidate his claim to be the conqueror of the Persian empire. Nevertheless, once he had captured Persepolis, Alexander had the problem of what to do with it. As it stood, Persepolis was a monument to the grandeur of the kings of Persia. Indeed, several were buried in impressive stone tombs carved into the rock face of the mountain that loomed over the city.

The last thing Alexander needed was a permanent reminder of the glory of the dynasty he had supplanted. So, in one drunken night, he and his retainers burned the city to the ground. Legend has it that this was an impromptu act of vandalism urged upon Alexander by a concubine who was still bitter about the Persian sack of her native city of Athens 150 years previously. However, the fact is that Alexander had got what he needed from Persepolis. He did not wish to use it as his own capital, and it could have become a symbol of Persian resistance. By burning the proud City of the Persians, Alexander demonstrated that the dynasty of Darius was vanquished once and for all, and that the empire was now under new management.

Oddly enough, this act of destruction also proved to be an act of preservation. The thousands of clay tablets in the royal archives were baked into ceramic by the heat of the fire. A partial collapse of the archive wall covered the records, which remained buried for the next 2,200 years. Unearthed in the early twentieth century, the tablets offer a unique snapshot of the administration of the provinces of the Persian empire in the years before it was overthrown.

Macedonians revel amid the blazing ruin of Persepolis in this 1890 painting by Georges-Antoine Rochegrosse. Modern historians believe that the destruction was not a drunken impulse but a calculated act of political symbolism.

Persepolis Today

Persepolis is now a UNESCO World Heritage Site. After its destruction, the city was left largely untouched until the excavations of modern archaeologists. As a result, the buildings and artefacts on the site are original and unreconstructed. Proud of its Persian heritage, the Iranian government is fiercely protective of the site, though it acknowledges some encroachments by agriculture and modern industrial development in the nearby town of Marvdasht.

Visitors to Persepolis often combine a visit (a day trip from the city of Shiraz) with a look at the impressive rock carvings of the tombs at Naqsh-e Rustam. There is an admittance charge to enter the site and guides are available (for a fee) to talk visitors through the history of Persepolis.

c. 600–133 BC
Numantia
'The Spanish Masada'

When supplies ran out … the weaker inhabitants became food.

Appian, *The Spanish Wars*

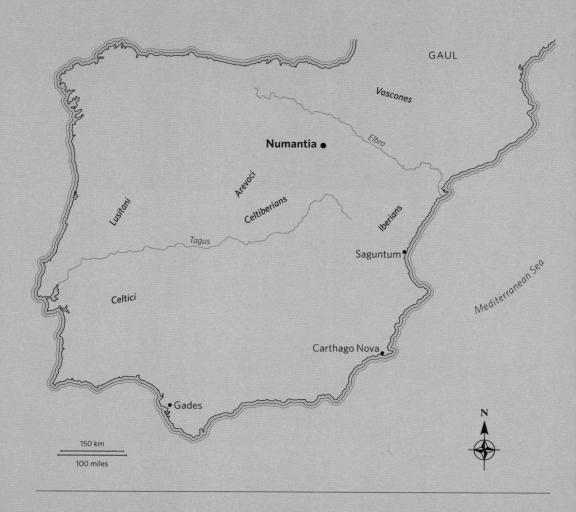

GAUL

Vascones

Numantia •

Elbro

Arevaci

Lusitani

Celtiberians

Iberians

Tagus

Saguntum •

Celtici

Mediterranean Sea

Carthago Nova •

• Gades

N

150 km

100 miles

Some time around 600 BC a new people appeared in the Iberian peninsula. From their language and artefacts it appears that the newcomers were Celts, but if so they quickly adapted to their new surroundings and formed a culture of their own, which today we call Celtiberian.

The ferocious and warlike Celtiberians quickly elbowed aside the previous occupants of the highlands of central Spain (which was no easy feat, as the original occupants were tough fighters in their own right). Around 300 BC the Celtiberians took over a settlement on a hill near the modern city of Soria and made it their own.

The site, on a hill today called the Cerro de la Muela ('Hill of the Tooth'), was an excellent location. The area was surrounded by dense forest, and a navigable river – the Douro – ran through the valley nearby. Decorations on contemporary pottery give a glimpse of the wildlife that was abundant in the area, with depictions of birds such as hoopoes, herons, eagles, partridges and doves.

Picture of Numantia from 1727 manuscript. The illustrator had to reconstruct his image from ancient descriptions, because the actual site of Numantia was only discovered 133 years later.

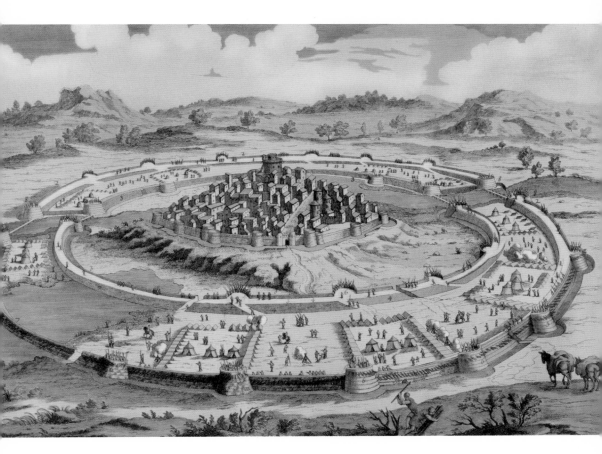

The actual site
of Numantia after
excavation in the
modern era. The
site is now a national
monument, and its
heroic defenders have
a revered place in
Spanish tradition.

The hilltop site controlled an ancient route along which shepherds
had, since time immemorial, driven their flocks and herds between
the Ebro Valley and the meadows beyond the Piqueras Pass. So
desirable was this location that modern archaeologists have found
signs that the hill was first occupied in the Late Neolithic era and
fortified in the more troubled times of the early Iron Age, beginning
around 900 BC. The last occupants were a branch of the Celtiberians
called the Arevaci, and they called their city Numantia.

Rome

The Celtiberians had gained their new home by forcing aside the
previous inhabitants, but had to defend it against a new breed of
invader. This was an enemy more organized and relentless than
any they had faced before – the senate and people of Rome.

Between 205 and 142 BC the Romans had humbled the might of
Carthage and conquered the Macedonian successors of Alexander

the Great. One might assume, therefore, that knocking over a few sparsely populated hillforts in the Spanish hinterland would not present much of a challenge. At this time the Numantines could probably muster five to eight thousand fighting men at most, while the legionaries of Rome were easily ten times that number. Yet the Spanish wars proved a massive headache for the Romans, and the stresses of the conflict caused fundamental changes in their society.

One of those changes is still with us today. In early Rome the year began in March, when the new consuls assumed office. Until the last years of the Roman Republic the consuls were also war leaders, and in the mid-second century BC one of the first jobs of a consul was to gather an army and march off to continue the apparently never-ending conquest of Iberia – a job that was finally wrapped up in the time of the emperor Augustus a century and a half later.

Because the campaigning season was mostly the spring and early summer (no sane person liked to fight in the Spanish heat of August), the consuls sometimes arrived just in time to turn around and go home. Therefore, it was decided to bring the start of the year forward to 1 January. This gave the consuls time to muster an army, march it to Spain and still have time to fight a decent campaign.

Even so, not many consuls managed a decent campaign. The Celtiberians and particularly the Numantines were a hard nut to crack. Contemporary Roman military formations were ill-equipped to deal with the hit-and-run tactics of their opponents in a country well suited for ambuscades and tricky for supply lines. In 136 BC a consul called Mancinus tried repeatedly to storm Numantia but was repeatedly repulsed.

After a particularly disastrous failure, Mancinus and his army were trapped and facing destruction. A young officer called Tiberius Gracchus, by some deft diplomacy, saved the legions and negotiated an equitable peace. This was promptly rejected by the Roman senate. Disowned by the Romans, Mancinus was delivered bound in chains to the gates of Numantia, but the Numantines refused to accept him. The disillusioned Tiberius Gracchus thereafter declared political war on Rome's self-serving political class, beginning a century of chaos that ended only with the fall of the Roman Republic itself.

War to the death

In 133 BC the Romans decided to deal with Numantia once and for all. They – for once – selected a competent general in Scipio Aemilianus and gave him a substantial army with which to finish the job. Scipio did not attempt to storm Numantia. 'The place was difficult to attack because of the river, ravines and thick woods around it', reports the historian Appian (*Spanish Wars* 16.76). 'There was only one road to open country, and that was blocked by ditches and barricades. Both as infantry and cavalry the Numantines were superb soldiers. Although they only numbered around eight thousand in all, their bravery caused the Romans considerable trouble.'

Modern excavations show that Numantia was located somewhat to the west of the hill crest and occupied an area of some 25 hectares (61 acres), the whole surrounded by a wall of mostly undressed stone so sturdy that in places it stands over 2 metres (6½ feet) high even today. Only two well-defended gates allowed access to the city, and Scipio wisely decided against a frontal attack. Instead, the Romans built a wall of their own, totally enclosing Numantia, and settled down to starve the inhabitants into submission.

The last days of Numantia were terrible, for the people refused to surrender. When the food ran out they began eating boiled leather, and then the bodies of the slain. When that source of sustenance failed, the weaker inhabitants became food for the stronger (says Appian, with the inference that the women and children were sacrificed to feed the fighting men).

When the Romans finally took Numantia they found the city almost depopulated, with the emaciated survivors weakened by plague and hunger. At the last, many committed suicide rather than fall into Roman hands. The Romans respected brave foes, but they also took firm measures to ensure that they never had to fight them again. Numantia was reduced to ashes, and the senate ordered that the city should never be rebuilt.

Roman Numantia

Yet rebuilt it was, for the site was too useful for the Romans of the imperial era to leave it abandoned. For the rest of the history of the Roman empire Numantia was an unremarkable Roman town with the status of a *municipium* (a city where the occupants had the rights and privileges of Romans). The city outgrew the original walls and spread out to the west and south, while the centre sprouted the usual Roman civic amenities – public baths (one for men and the other for women), a monumental arch and a public portico.

Nevertheless, Roman Numantia declined along with the Roman empire and was barely inhabited in the fourth century. There are signs that Spain's Visigothic conquerors briefly occupied the site in the sixth century, but thereafter Numantia was abandoned and the site was forgotten.

Twin horses face away from each other on this decoration from the necropolis at Numantia. This was designed to fit atop a staff and may have been a symbol of office.

Numantia Today

The Fall of Numantia by Alejo Vera, 1881. Grim as the depiction here might be, the reality was probably even more so. Rather than committing suicide in the face of attacking Roman troops, many of the women had already been slain – and eaten – by the defenders.

Yet memory of Numantia and the desperate last stand of its inhabitants remained. In the Middle Ages, Numantia became a symbol of national unity, promoted by the monarchy at León. The site of the lost city was originally thought to be at Zamora in Castile, but the proper location was discovered in 1860.

The site is now a national monument replete with memorials erected at different times in the modern era to commemorate that last stand – which has also become embedded in colloquial Spanish. A *defensa Numantina* now refers to any stubborn, last-ditch defence and is popular with, for example, sports commentators.

PART THREE

Across the Roman Empire

The cities of the Roman era described here fall into two categories – those created, and those lost. That a large number of settlements were lost, especially in northwestern Europe, should be no surprise. The Romans and the peoples they conquered were at different stages in the developing concept of urbanism, and the Romans had no hesitation in bringing their new subjects up to date with their idea of what a city should be. This was done in large part by encouraging the population to abandon cities that differed from their preferred model and to move into more 'suitable' custom-built cities.

This policy was highly successful – so much so that, in many ways, the Roman concept of the city remains with us today. That concept became fundamentally ingrained in Western culture, as demonstrated by the number of civic buildings, from courthouses to libraries, that echo Roman architectural style. The Romans saw their empire as a mosaic of such *civitates* – each a semi-autonomous administrative region, with a city at its heart, from which the villages and farms of the surrounding countryside were taxed and organized. (The means of such organization dated back to the independent Greek *poleis* – the city-states which have given us the word 'politics'.) The modern, much weaker, equivalent of a *civitas* is probably 'county'.

Urbs et Orbis

Surprisingly, a substantial population was not among the criteria that defined a Roman city as a city. A city was the administrative centre for the surrounding countryside. In Europe, this hinterland had often belonged to a particular tribe, so the city – which was sometimes a pre-existing tribal centre, sometimes a new foundation – became the urban manifestation of that tribe. Two outstanding examples in the modern world are the tribal centres of the Parisii and the Veneti.

For the purposes of Roman administration certain structures were necessary, principally a basilica for the administration of justice and the keeping of records. Those people who still considered that the primary function of a city was defence were lured from their cramped and draughty hillforts by such modern amenities as sewers, fountains and bathhouses. (When the Romans started a city from scratch, proper drainage and watercourses were among the first things to be constructed.)

For Rome, one major purpose of a city was that it should help bring a conquered people into the Roman world. By and large, Romanization was not purely an enforced process of cultural colonization, but also a gentler melding of Roman attributes into the local culture. One aspect of this was the building of temples celebrating local gods as aspects of Greco-Roman divinities. Nevertheless, it was stressed that an individual's degree of 'civilization' was measured by the extent to which he or she subscribed to Greco-Roman ideals. To aid this process, Roman-built cities had theatres, libraries and amphitheatres. City walls were often used for administrative purposes as much as for defence, allowing the authorities to keep track of who and what was entering and leaving the city.

This model of urban culture was widespread across the empire, and nowhere more than in the cities that the Romans called 'colonies'. A *colonia* was not simply a Roman outpost; it was regarded as an extension of the city of Rome itself, and its citizens shared the same rights and obligations as those living in the shadow of the Palatine. As a result of this homogenization of urban culture, a visitor from, say, Timgad in the North African interior could feel as much at home in Caesaraugusta (Zaragoza, Spain) as in Colonia Claudia Ara Agrippinensium (Cologne, Germany) or Caesarea (Caesarea, Israel).

The world according to Rome

Thus we see in the Roman world a particular concept of the city. By this interpretation, cities did not grow organically, from hamlet, to village, to town and so on. Instead, a city was founded by design, at a carefully selected location, for reasons that might be economic, military or cultural. Cities were remarkably similar, wherever in the Greco-Roman world they were located, and contained many of the same amenities. While the empire stood this was a highly successful model, and many Roman foundations remain thriving cities today. However, by the fourth century AD the world was changing, and many of the lost and forgotten cities in the fourth and final section of this book are those which failed to survive the transition.

c. 600 BC–AD 275

Glanum

Sacred City in Gaul

Divine vengeance descended upon the town in the year AD 275.

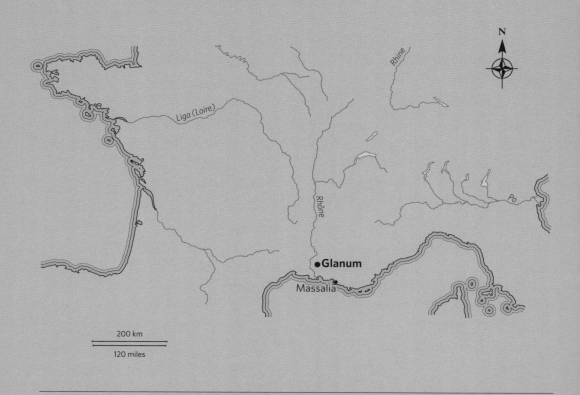

There was a sacred spring at the site of Glanum even before an Iron Age Gallic tribe called the Salluvii moved into the area around 600 BC. The tribesmen were attracted to the site not only by its religious significance but also by the conjunction of the spring and a highly defensible nearby hilltop. It helped that the hill overlooked a valley, now known as Notre-Dame-de-Laval, on the main trading route from the coast to the interior of what is now Provence in southern France.

The trading opportunities were also noted by those inveterate colonists, the Greeks. At this time the people of Phocaea in Asia Minor were being threatened by the expanding empire of the Achaemenid Persians, and many of them packed up and moved as far away from Persia as they could get. They founded Massalia (later Marseilles) on the coast at around the same time that the Gauls founded Glanum inland. It was not long before some enterprising Greeks from Massalia moved further up the trade corridor to set up shop in Glanum, and thereafter the histories of the two cities – among the oldest in France – remained permanently interlinked.

Extensive weathering has made it hard to distinguish the protagonists of this battle scene on the Mausoleum of the Julii. The monument, erected at the end of the first century BC, honoured the ancestors of the Julian family members who commissioned it.

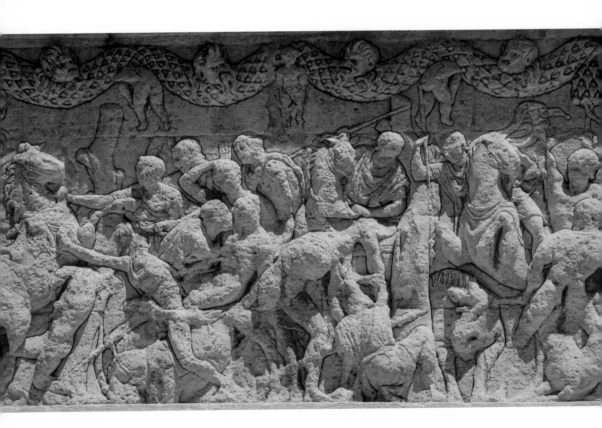

The Gallo-Greek city

A Hellenistic quarter developed in the city and successful traders built themselves impressive villas, while other houses in the Greek style were built around them. One of these, the 'House of the Antae', named for the pillars set on either side of the main doorway, is still in a state of remarkable preservation that testifies to the skill of the original architect. The two-storey building was built around a natural pool, fed by rainwater artfully channelled down from the roof. In another house the colourful floor mosaics still remain where once the host might have thrown a drinking symposium for others in the trading community. Despite this Greekification, other aspects of Glanum remained firmly Gallic. A quick study of the site's cooking vessels suggests that the inhabitants boiled their vegetables (as northerners still do), rather than frying them in olive oil, as Mediterranean peoples preferred (and still prefer).

The House of the Antae from the residential district in Glanum. Tuscan-style columns form a peristyle around a central atrium with a pool.

The sacred spring remained a major feature of the town, which took its name from the spring's patron deity, Glanis, and the three associated mother-goddesses (called Glanicae). Special pools were created in which pilgrims could bathe, and a prominent altar to Glanis was set up behind the wall that encircled the sacred site. A flight of thirty-seven steps led down from one temple to a

2-metre-wide (6½-foot) well of holy water, and it is probable that the temple contained votive offerings and dedications from those who had benefited from Glanis's healing powers. By the second century BC Glanum was prosperous enough to issue its own currency – silver coins featuring a bull and one of the Glanic mother goddesses.

Some 20 hectares (50 acres) of the town were protected by a circuit wall, though this did not extend far enough to cover another ancient religious site – an early Iron Age sanctuary to the south. The walls were made of the abundant native limestone, which was also the base material for the buildings of the town.

There were two major threats to the city's prosperity. The first was Massalia, perhaps now envious of the increasing wealth of Glanum. The second was the growing power of a people who had barely existed when Glanum was founded – the warlike and expansionist Romans. The Massilots allied themselves with these newcomers, and at the end of the second century BC the Salluvii suffered a crushing defeat at Roman hands. The city was captured and many of its monumental features destroyed.

Roman Glanum

In 90 BC Rome fell out with its Italian allies (the *socii*) and came close to defeat in what is today called the Social War. The Salluvii took this opportunity to try to throw off Roman rule, but their rebellion was ultimately crushed by a Roman army, which came close to destroying Glanum altogether. However, the convenient location of the site, its abundant water and the sacred spring all helped to preserve the city. In fact, trade flourished as the Roman road to the Gallic interior, the Via Domitia, later ran through the town.

By the start of the Roman imperial era in the first century AD, Glanum was again a flourishing little city. As was the Roman habit, the local god was not cast down, but conflated with similar gods in the Roman pantheon: Glanis became Valetudo, who was herself a reimagining of the Greek goddess Hygieia – that deity who has given us the modern concept of hygiene. Thermal baths and a swimming pool supplemented the bathing area beside the sacred spring.

The needs of the expanding population were met by the building of two small aqueducts and a curved, stone-arched dam, which helped to supply water to the town's abundant fountains. Waste water was removed by an efficient system of Roman sewers and drains. A new forum sprang up in the centre of town, built over – and partly with – the remnants of the Hellenistic-era buildings and monuments that had once stood there.

Statue of a captive Gaul, excavated at Glanum. Appropriately enough, this tightly bound figure is now among the exhibits at the Hotel de Sade, built upon the remains of Roman baths in nearby Saint-Rémy.

The houses from the period, with their rich frescoes and mosaics, speak of a prosperous community. A bustling market centre fuelled by trade supplemented the usual business of a Roman city, which served as a centre of administration (*civitas*) for the people of the surrounding countryside. New and more impressive monuments were built during the imperial period, several commemorating Roman emperors and the cult of their worship. A U-shaped building with an impressive colonnade now surrounded the sacred spring.

Decline and fall

The fortunes of Glanum changed as the Roman empire became Christian. The sacred well seems to have been used as a rubbish tip. Perhaps through outrage at this treatment, divine vengeance descended upon the town in the year AD 275. A horde of plundering Alemanni barbarians fell upon Glanum and largely destroyed it.

With Glanum no longer a cult centre, there was no reason to stay put, so the residents re-established themselves at what is now Saint-Rémy-de-Provence, about a kilometre (½ mile) to the north. Without human intervention to control it, mud and silt washed down from the ridge where the first settlement had been almost a thousand years before. Over the course of the centuries the abandoned Greco-Roman city of Glanum was gradually buried and largely forgotten.

Glanum Today

During the Renaissance there was new interest in the Greek and Roman heritage of France, and Glanum was partially excavated, mainly in the hunt for interesting sculptures and coins. Serious archaeology began in the early nineteenth century and has continued since, interrupted only by another Germanic invasion in 1941.

Visitors can tour most of the ancient city, and view some impressive surviving monuments. Among these is the 'Mausoleum of the Julii', a largely intact 18-metre-tall (59½-foot) cenotaph erected by the family of a man granted Roman citizenship by Augustus. The bas-reliefs on the base show battles and scenes from mythology. A triumphal arch stands at the north gate of the city, through which tourists can pass to visit other monuments near the ancient forum.

As a bonus, those making the trip from Saint-Rémy can stay at a hotel built upon fourth-century Roman baths. This hotel was once the family home of the town's most notorious resident, the Marquis de Sade.

241 BC–*c*. AD 550
Falerii Novi
Explored but not Excavated

Excavations at Falerii Novi represent
the cutting edge of archaeological science.

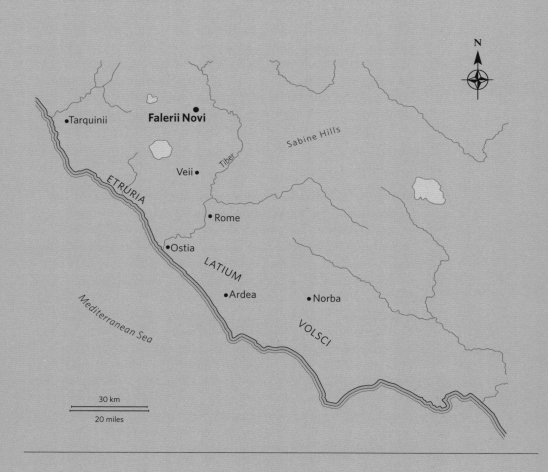

W hile the origins of many lost cities are shrouded by the mists of time, we know the foundation date of Falerii Novi. The Romans set up the city, and they were quite precise about such matters. (If we are to believe the Roman account – and nobody has disproven it yet – Rome itself was founded in 753 BC, on 21 April, shortly before eleven o'clock in the morning.)

Falerii Novi ('New Falerni') was founded in the summer of 241 BC, at the same time that Falerii Veteres ('Old Falerni') was abandoned. The link between these two events was a short but brutal war fought between the Faliscans and the expanding power of Rome. The Faliscans were a Latin people who lived right on the border of Etruria and had close links with many Etruscan allies.

The historians Livy and Polybius record that the war consisted of two battles and a siege. The first battle was a losing draw for the Romans, the second a decisive victory, and the siege a three-day

'Jupiter's Gate', with the head of a divinity carved above the keystone of the gate arch. Arrivals in the classical era would have seen a bustling city behind the gate – a city now resting undisturbed beneath the trees.

event that led to Faliscan surrender. The Romans confiscated half of the tribe's territory, but by way of compensation built them a brand-new city. This was located on the plain a few kilometres away from the uncomfortable rocky spur upon which Falerii Veteres was perched.

The new city

The Romans were not being altogether altruistic in building a new home for the conquered people. The Faliscans were located a mere 50 kilometres (31 miles) north of Rome itself, and if the tribe had not been so demoralized by their defeat on the battlefield, the siege of Falerii Veteres would have been a far tougher affair. Falerii Novi was a much less defensible proposition, but – as the Romans doubtless informed the dubious new inhabitants – one does not need a fortress when one's defence is managed by the legions of Rome.

Nevertheless, in case the city should need to be defended before the legions arrived, the Romans built a substantial wall, over 2 kilometres (1¼ miles) in length, and studded it with some fifty turrets. This wall was so well built that it has endured for over two thousand years, often with minimal maintenance.

The site of Falerii Novi was not entirely unoccupied; there was already a substantial temple at the location. This may have been dedicated to the god Dionysus, as one of the few relics unearthed from the site (and now in the Louvre) is related to his cult. The Romans started by methodically laying out roads and putting down water pipes, and then building a market area with a theatre backing on to it, and constructing a larger amphitheatre outside the walls. Once the city was ready for occupation, the people of Falerii Veteres were resettled in their new home.

The end

Falerii Novi became a perfectly ordinary Italian city, bypassed by history for the next thousand years. The population farmed the surrounding fields, traded in the market and took time off at the theatre and in the baths. Like the Roman empire in its prime, Falerii Novi seemed prosperous and largely content. However, the city was very much a product of the empire, and when Rome fell, Falerii Novi went down with it.

The city had been deliberately located in a poor defensive position, and when the barbarian hordes came calling the population moved away. In fact they moved back to Falerii Veteres – and their descendants remain there still in the community of Città Castellana. Falerii Novi was left to decay and the ruins were eventually buried by the passage of time. A Benedictine abbey was built near the west gate in the eleventh century – partly from stones taken from the city's ruins. Otherwise, the city's substantial walls became a magnificent fence for a farm, where corn and figs are grown today.

Rediscovering Falerii Novi

Because the city walls survived, it required no great feat of deduction to conclude that there had once been a city within, and in 1820 the first of a succession of amateur archaeologists arrived on the site. This prompted the Vatican (which now owned part of the property) to issue an edict that discoveries at Falerii Novi could not be taken away for display in other parts of Europe – the first-ever law on cultural patrimony, which has since been widely replicated elsewhere.

Bust of a woman wearing aristocratic clothing – possibly a depiction of Ariadne, wife of Bacchus. Discovered at Falerii Novi in 1829, this statue is now in the Louvre, France.

In more recent years Falerii Novi has moved to the cutting edge of archaeology. One problem with excavating ancient ruins is that, once excavated, they require considerable maintenance lest they deteriorate further. Given that maintenance is often a low priority for administrations facing other, urgent financial demands, many ancient ruins would have benefited considerably from never having been brought to light in the first place.

The site of Falerii Novi is flat, and has no modern buildings on top of it, making it an excellent test bed for non-intrusive archaeological techniques. The earliest of these was aerial photography. Observing a site from above in the right light conditions can reveal bumps and hollows that follow the outlines of buried roads and buildings.

The British School at Rome followed the initial aerial survey up with a scan of the entire site using LIDAR (Light Detection and Ranging) and within a few years improved upon their findings with the use of magnetometry – the first time this technology had been used upon a site in Italy. By now the site was well mapped, with the location of the roads and major buildings established, while the surface remained an undisturbed cornfield.

More recently the site has been scanned again, this time by researchers from the Universities of Cambridge and Ghent,

who used ground-penetrating radar. This technique allowed the archaeologists to scan to different depths, and thus go through layer after layer of the city's history. The pioneering techniques used at Falerii Novi have huge implications for archaeology. They allow ruins to be explored without being excavated, even the remains of ancient cities that have modern cities on top of them (complete with inhabitants unwilling to accommodate archaeologists intent on excavating their basements).

Falerii Novi Today

Many Italian archaeological sites have more immediate appeal to the historically minded tourist, who is not looking for relaxation beside a bucolic cornfield. However, the walls of Falerii Novi bear investigation, especially two remarkably well-preserved gates. These are now called the Gateway of the Ox and the Gateway of Jupiter, after the bas-reliefs on each. (The carving of Jupiter is a copy of the original, which is now safely housed in a museum.)

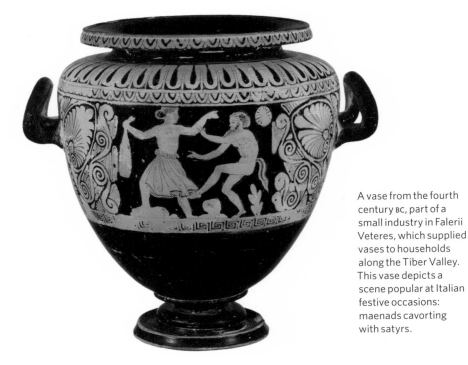

A vase from the fourth century BC, part of a small industry in Falerii Veteres, which supplied vases to households along the Tiber Valley. This vase depicts a scene popular at Italian festive occasions: maenads cavorting with satyrs.

630 BC–AD 643
Cyrene
Greek City on the Egyptian Border

Ruled by Cleopatra Selene, daughter of Cleopatra of Egypt and Mark Antony.

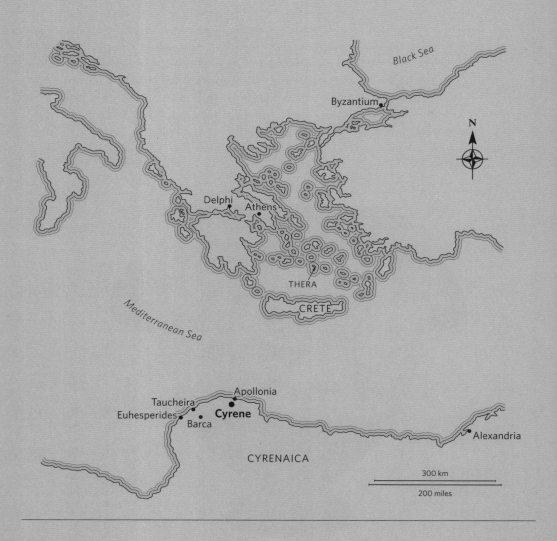

Around 700 BC, a native of the Greek island of Thera consulted the Oracle at Delphi. The famed Pythia – the far-seeing priestess of Apollo – informed this man that he urgently needed to 'found a city in Libya'. This advice was ignored, reports the historian Herodotus (*History* 4.150ff), mainly because nobody on Thera had any idea where Libya was.

A seven-year drought helped to focus minds, and in due course a party of colonists departed to explore the land to the south. The original Greek settlement in Libya was unsatisfactory, partly because of friction with the locals, and eventually (the traditional date is 630 BC) a treaty agreement led to the Greeks settling in a lush valley in what is today the Jebel Akhdar upland. This settlement was some 14 kilometres (8¾ miles) from the sea, an arrangement which was not unusual in the days of large pirate fleets with a predilection for raiding coastal cities.

Just as Rome (founded inland partly for the same reason) had Ostia, and Athens had the Piraeus, the new settlement developed a port, which the people called Apollonia in honour of the god who had brought them there. The inland city probably named itself after a spring called Keres, which the Greeks immediately dedicated to Apollo and made the main source of the municipal water supply. Later mythologers retrofitted the story of Apollo with a lover called Cyrene and decided that the city was named after her.

Cast around 2,300 years ago, this bronze appears to be a portrait sculpture of a young man of Cyrene. The facial features, moustache and light beard suggest that the subject was of Berber stock.

A thriving city

'The city flourished because the soil was excellent and the crops fine. The region is particularly suitable for breeding horses', reported the Roman geographer Strabo (*Geography* 17.3.21) as he explained the rapid growth of Cyrene thereafter. Under King Battus III ('the Fortunate') there was a further surge in colonization, mostly at the expense of the local peoples. Cyrene was now joined by three other Greek colonies on the coast: Euhesperides (modern Benghazi), Taucheira and Barca. Along with the port city of Apollonia, the whole group became known in antiquity as the 'Cyrenaican Pentapolis' – the five cities of the region of Cyrene.

One reason for the rapid development of the region was the discovery and intensive cultivation of a plant called silphium. This provided a natural and reasonably safe abortifacient, which alone would have made it much in demand in the ancient world, and had other medicinal uses. For gourmet cooks, silphium made a

Mosaic floor of the house of Jason Magnus, a priest of Apollo at Cyrene. The female statues in the background wear the peplos, a traditional dress of heavy linen.

splendid vegetable dish. Despite efforts to grow silphium elsewhere, the plant stubbornly refused to flourish anywhere but in its native soil. Exports of the crop so helped the prosperity of the city that an image of the heart-shaped silphium seed came to identify the coinage of Cyrene, rather as owls typify the coinage of Athens.

One measure of Cyrene's prosperity can be seen in the remains of a massive temple to Zeus, which was constructed on the north side of the city, near to another grandiose temple to the city's patron god, Apollo.

Ever since the third century BC Cyrene had also been famed as a centre of learning and philosophy. The school of philosophy was founded by one Aristippus, a student of Socrates. The Cyrenaic philosophers taught that finding pleasure in socially acceptable ways should be considered the greatest good. Other more practically minded types founded schools of architecture and medicine.

Hellenistic Cyrene

The expanding power and influence of Cyrenaica naturally brought the region to the attention of the neighbouring Egyptians. Perhaps fortunately for the cities of the Pentapolis, the Egyptians had problems of their own with the Persians, a people with whom the Cyrenaicans were careful to remain on good terms. This preserved a precarious independence for the city, which was quashed with the arrival of the armies of Alexander the Great.

A general called Ophellas took command of the city, nominally in the name of his Macedonian overlords. However, Ophellas quickly realized that the shambolic state of Alexander's conquests allowed him almost complete autonomy, and his successors leveraged this autonomy into independence. In 276 BC one Magas crowned himself king of Cyrenaica and went so far as to (unsuccessfully) invade Egypt. Thereafter Cyrene maintained an uneasy and unstable peace with the Ptolemies, who gradually came to dominate the city.

Among the colourful characters of the Hellenistic era of Cyrene was Queen Berenice II. She married a Macedonian noble called Demetrius the Fair, who was so handsome that Berenice's mother had an affair with him. Berenice, who was known to have ridden with her father into battle, put a bloody end to that romance by having assassins kill her husband in her mother's bedchamber, while she stood in the doorway critiquing their work. Berenice went on to enter a prize-winning chariot team at the Olympic Games (by one dubious report, she drove the team herself) and she eventually married Ptolemy III of Egypt.

At this time the greatest scholar from Cyrene was one Eratosthenes, a mathematician and friend of Archimedes who went on to work at the Library of Alexandria. He is best known today for calculating the circumference of the world, which he reckoned at 250,000 *stadia* – and depending which measurement of the *stade* one uses, he was between a hundred and a thousand miles out. That's partly because the Earth is not a perfect sphere, being somewhat fatter at the equator, and partly because there were different measures for a *stade* in antiquity and it is uncertain which Eratosthenes employed in his calculations.

Roman Cyrene

In 96 BC the last king of Cyrene, Ptolemy Apion, died without an heir and bequeathed his kingdom to Rome. (This form of bequest was not unprecedented; it could protect an insecure king from assassination by would-be successors.) During the Roman civil wars that followed the rebellion and assassination of Julius Caesar, Cyrene briefly became independent again under the rule of Cleopatra Selene, the daughter of Cleopatra of Egypt and her lover Mark Antony.

In the early imperial era Cyrene was already somewhat in decline, as a changing climate and over-farming had made the silphium plant extinct. (One of the last plants was given as a curiosity to the emperor Nero.) The city had a large Jewish population, who were caught up in more widespread rebellions against Rome in AD 70 and 117. The unrest in Cyrene was suppressed ruthlessly by the Romans, with substantial loss of life. We also hear in the Gospels of another Cyrenaican Jew, Simon of Cyrene, who was in Jerusalem for the Passover when he was pressed into service to help Jesus carry his cross to Golgotha.

Without the advantage of its silphium crop, Cyrene was unable to compete with Carthage and Alexandria as a trading port, and the city began to fail economically. It was then hit by a series of devastating earthquakes in the third century, after which the demoralized populace made little attempt to rebuild. By the time of the late Roman empire, the historian Ammianus Marcellinus described the city as abandoned.

In fact, a remnant of the once-thriving city held on until AD 643, when it was attacked by desert nomads during the confusion of the Arab conquest. Thereafter Cyrene ceased to be inhabited.

The Apollo of Cyrene. Identified by the snake and his kithara-style lyre, Apollo's statue was reconstructed from some 120 pieces found scattered around the original pedestal. One arm remains missing.

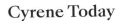

Cyrene Today

The ruins of the ancient city are now partly covered by the modern settlement of Shahhat. Much of what remains is in poor condition after being picked over by looters and nineteenth-century archaeologists (insofar as these two were different). Nor has preservation of ancient Cyrene been helped by the modern war between factions which, at the time of writing, still splutters on in Libya.

Nevertheless, some superb Greco-Roman statuary has emerged from the ruins and some progress had, until recent decades, been made in excavating the site. UNESCO has made it a World Heritage Site, but one at considerable risk. Doubtless researchers will return to Cyrene as soon as it becomes practicable, and what was once one of the most opulent cities of the Mediterranean world may then give up more of its secrets.

c. 850 BC–AD 700
Tipasa
Cosmopolitan Trade Centre

*Cargoes of olives, ivory and exotic beasts
in cages were stacked on the wharves.*

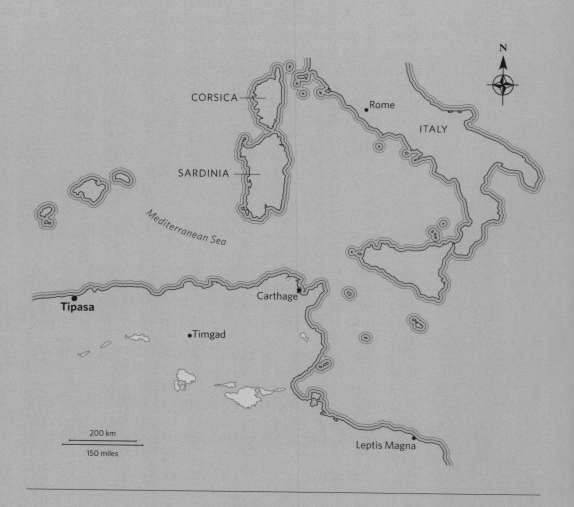

Much of the beauty that attracted settlers to the site of Tipasa three thousand years ago remains today. The golden beaches of the bay spread out between a blue sea and rolling hills covered with pine trees. The first settlers quickly established olive groves, and these are still a feature of the area.

Originally Tipasa was a trading post. Lying on the coast of present-day Algeria, it was conveniently positioned for merchants, whose ships ran before the prevailing winds to harbours in Sicily, Spain and Italy. Tipasa was also a handy jumping-off point for those heading inland into what was then the prosperous kingdom of Mauretania. This location, at a nexus of early Mediterranean trade, is what gave Tipasa its name, which means 'crossing place'.

Phoenician and Hellenistic Tipasa

The first people to call Tipasa home were Phoenicians, the same people who founded Carthage further down the coast to the east. (The relatively recent foundation of Carthage is shown in that

Ruins of the Basilica of St Salsa, overlooking the sea. St Salsa (both the saint and the dance get their name from the Latin for 'sauce') was a teenage girl who was martyred for destroying one of the town's venerated pagan monuments.

Tipasa's scenic, coastal location was one of the city's delights, but high tides and storms might destroy its remains.

Tipasa's scenic, coastal location was one of the city's delights, but high tides and storms might destroy its remains.

city's name, which means 'New Town'.) Houses of the local honey-coloured stone were built on a low bluff overlooking a sheltered anchorage in the bay, and thereafter Tipasa was open for business. Not only did the town serve as a way-station for travellers from all over the Mediterranean, but it quickly became the chosen venue for local traders looking to bring native wares to a larger market.

Today we know of these first settlers from their tombs, for Tipasa has one of the oldest and most extensive Phoenician burial sites in the western Mediterranean. The sailors and traders buried here had diverse tombs and funerary practices, showing influences from

Greece, Italy, Iberia and even the great civilizations of Mesopotamia as well as the local North African culture.

Later, Tipasa came under the influence of Hellenistic settlers when the Phoenician cities in the Levant were subsumed into the empire of Alexander the Great in the 330s BC. This added a Greek flavour to the Semitic tone of the original trading settlement – which already had a strong local tinge. The embodiment of this multicultural melange can still be seen in the highly impressive tomb of one of the last Ptolemaic queens, Cleopatra Selene, the daughter of Cleopatra VII and the Roman triumvir Mark Antony.

By 20 BC Cleopatra Selene was married to King Juba II of Numidia to cement a diplomatic alliance between Egypt and this part of North Africa. Evidently the royal couple spent a considerable amount of time at Tipasa, as this is where they chose to be buried. Interestingly, their mausoleum is not only similar to other burial places in ancient Numidia, but also bears a very strong resemblance to the mausoleum that Augustus designed for himself in Rome. Since we know that Juba visited Augustus – who had taken Cleopatra Selene as a captive after conquering Egypt – in Rome, there is an intriguing possibility that the pair discussed their personal funerary arrangements.

The tomb in Tipasa is given added prominence in that its 30-metre-high (98-foot) conical structure is set atop a hill, some 250 metres (820 feet) above the beach. The building has now endured two thousand years of weathering, but much of its present dilapidation is due to humans. Plunderers ripped through looking for hidden treasure, and once everything of value had gone (including the marble columns that once surrounded the base) the edifice appears to have served as a family home. If Juba and Cleopatra were buried there, the remains of the dead were ejected to make room for the living and the tomb is now empty.

Roman Tipasa

Following pages
The impressive remains of the royal mausoleum at Tipasa. Built for King Juba, a friend of the emperor Augustus, and Cleopatra Selene, daughter of Cleopatra of Egypt, it is uncertain whether this edifice was designed as a tomb or a memorial.

When the expanding Roman empire took over the North African littoral, Tipasa added a new layer to its cosmopolitan structure. Typically Roman features were installed, including baths, a basilica and an amphitheatre for the public entertainment of a population that probably numbered some twenty thousand. The city remained an important station on the international maritime trade routes, but the Romans also made it a central node in the network of roads that they were building across that part of Africa.

The roads made it easier for local goods to be brought to market, and in the Roman era large-scale agriculture took off around the

city, and many Roman villas were built. The city grew as the Roman empire prospered, reaching its greatest extent in the second and third centuries AD. A defensive wall that was over 2 kilometres (1¼ miles) in length was erected to protect this important centre of trade from Berber raids.

By this time, Tipasa was officially a Roman colony. The people of Colonia Aelia Augusta Tipasensium – to give the city the full Roman name bestowed upon it in the mid-Antonine period (AD 117–161) – were Roman citizens with full rights. Also in this period the emperor Hadrian's successor, Antoninus Pius, ordered the rebuilding of Tipasa's walls on an even grander scale.

The anchorage by the beach would have been thronged with merchants, with cargoes of olives, ivory and exotic beasts in cages stacked on the wharves. The market in the forum would have been packed with camels, donkeys and farm animals such as goats and chickens, many awaiting on-board consumption by hungry sailors. The seamen themselves might be North African, Greek, Syrian, Gallic or Italian. Housing and villa complexes stretched along the shores of the bay to the slopes of Mount Chenoua – the dominant geographical feature on the western side. The walled city lay mostly on the central bluff, the whole covering more than 70 hectares (173 acres).

Later Tipasa

A fresh crop of buildings signalled the coming of Christianity in the later empire – the first Christian inscriptions date to AD 238 – including a large basilica with paved mosaic floors. Little else of the basilica survives, because, as with many other Roman remains, the structure was used as a source of building stone by later locals. The pride of Christian Tipasa was St Salsa, who was martyred by indignant townsfolk after she not only protested against the rites honouring the local god, but also threw the cult statue into the sea.

As the *Pax Romana* began to crumble, the walls of Tipasa were tested by a local rebel whose forces overran a number of other nearby cities, including Icosium, 70 kilometres (43½ miles) away, which became the modern city of Algiers. The Romans used Tipasa as their base when they set about suppressing the rebellion, but half a century later, in 430, the barbarian Vandal tribe took the city and Tipasa's prosperity came to a brutal end.

The Byzantines reconquered much of North Africa, but paid little attention to Tipasa, and the city's few forlorn Byzantine structures rapidly joined the rest of the city in falling into neglected ruins that

The basilica of Tipasa was used for commerce, administration and judicial affairs. The latter role probably inspired its mosaic floor of the second century AD. Called the 'Mosaic of the Captives', it is unknown who the nine individuals around the central image might be.

were slowly buried beneath sand and debris. By the time of the Muslim conquest of AD 1100, Tipasa was barely a memory.

Tipasa Today

Tipasa sprang back to life as a village in the 1850s and today is the large town of Tipaza. Many of the ruins of the old city were protected through the centuries beneath up to 4 metres (13 feet) of debris, but changing sea levels have damaged some sites near the ancient waterline, and storm surges brought on by an increasingly violent climate are endangering much of what remains.

In the early years of Tipasa's resettlement, new housing encroached upon the ancient ruins, a problem compounded by the first Western tourists, who took advantage of unrestricted access to the site to help themselves to souvenirs.

Like many a rediscovered city, Tipasa is now a UNESCO World Heritage Site, and two archaeological parks protect much of what remains. Sadly, it might be harder to hold back the waves of an increasingly destructive sea. The beautiful seashore location which led to Tipasa's founding three thousand years ago might yet prove the city's undoing.

c. 500 BC–AD 500
Baiae
Sin City

Degenerate Baiae whose beaches ... have long been the ruin of decent girls ...

Propertius, *Elegies* 1.11 l. 27

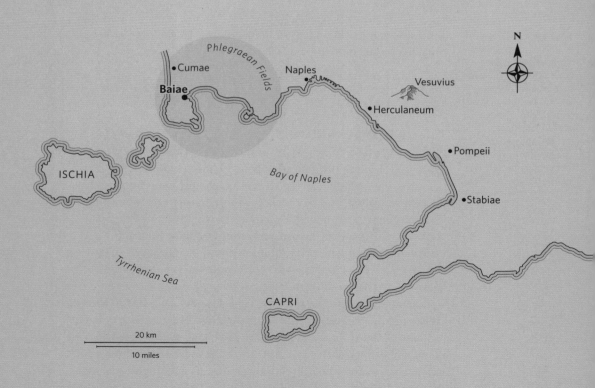

Perhaps the poet Propertius might not have enjoyed Baiae, but many Romans certainly did. Caesar had a mansion there, as did Pompey, Marius and almost everyone of note in the late Republic. It was the kind of place, remarked the Roman satirist Martial in his *Epigrams* (1.62), where a woman would arrive a Penelope (the famously chaste wife of Ulysses) and leave a Helen (the adulterous wife of Menelaus who ran off to Troy with her lover).

Baiae was said to have been named after the helmsman of the ship of Ulysses, a man called Baius, who drowned in the nearby

Mercury watched over those who took the waters at the Baths of Sosandra. This complex underwent several renovations over the centuries it was in use. Most of the elaborate sculpture and mosaics found here date to the second century AD, some 250 years after the baths were first built.

bay. However, the location had an even older connection with mythology. Baiae stands on top of a super-volcano, Campi Flegrei, which is still bubbling away and threatening the citizens of nearby Naples. In antiquity this area was called the Phlegraean Fields, and the volcanic grumblings were supposed to be caused by monsters from the dawn of time who were trapped underground after an epic battle with the Olympian gods.

Beginnings

Volcanic activity has created a number of hot springs around the bay, and this naturally warm sulphuric water was channelled into a number of baths and swimming pools for the benefit of visitors. From there, what had started as a modest fishing port around 500 BC and then grown into the port of the nearby city of Cumae now began to develop into one of the world's earliest pleasure resorts. (The island of Canopus in Ptolemaic Egypt has a good claim to being the first.)

In the 170s BC the resort was known as the Aquae Cumanae – the Cumaean Waters – and, indeed, it never gained full city status in its own right. Baiae was always technically an administrative district of Cumae. In the early years a visit to the resort was seen as good for the body rather than bad for the soul. Even that avid chronicler of Roman decadence, the poet Ovid, praised the resort's waters in his guide to seduction, the *Ars Amatoria* (1.8): 'Consider beautiful Baiae with its springs of smoking sulphur and the bay adorned with sails.'

Seductions were common enough in Baiae, causing the poet Propertius in 25 BC to write plaintively to his love:

> Hurry out of degenerate Baiae
> Whose beaches bring divorce to many
> And have long been the ruin of decent girls.
> Baiae's accursed waters, love's disgrace!
> (*Elegies* 1.11)

Being around 150 kilometres (90 miles) from Rome itself, Baiae was convenient for those wanting to get out of the big city, for one reason or another. Notoriously, some young Roman women took the waters in Baiae for up to nine months, and returned home somewhat slimmer but with their reputations intact.

Baiae was a resort for the rich, and many built splendid mansions jutting out into the waters of the bay or on the hilltops overlooking the town. (Julius Caesar sojourned in one such hilltop dwelling, and it was there that the emperor Hadrian breathed his last, some two centuries later.) Modern archaeologists investigating the remains of the beach-front properties have noted that the mansions were designed to be viewed from the sea by those on passing pleasure barges.

Imperial Baiae

In the imperial period Baiae's reputation only increased (or decreased, depending on one's perspective). The low opinion of Seneca, Nero's adviser, did not stop that emperor from having a splendid palace in Baiae. It was there that Nero entertained his mother at a dinner party, before sending her home in a boat designed to sink and drown her. (Politics were involved. The mother swam ashore, but was finished off with a sword.)

The seer Thrasyllus once remarked that Caligula was 'more likely to cross the bay of Baiae in a chariot than become emperor'. Accordingly, having become emperor, Caligula rounded up pleasure barges to make a 5-kilometre (3-mile) pontoon bridge, laid planking over it and did indeed drive a chariot across the bay (Suetonius, *Caligula* 19).

In the second century some of the most imposing buildings of the resort were constructed, including the 'temples' of Venus and Diana. The ruins of these structures can be viewed by tourists today, although closer investigation has revealed that the buildings were, in fact, elaborate bath complexes. Indeed, one building contained what seems to have been an early casino.

As the empire became more Christian and strait-laced Baiae lost its popular appeal and sank into decline. Indeed, some of the last recorded visitors were barbarian Visigoths and Vandals, sampling the delights of civilization before going on to wreck its foundations. What the barbarians left standing was destroyed by Muslim raiders in the eighth century, but the final blow to the resort was dealt not by humans but malaria-carrying mosquitoes. These became so bad that by AD 1500 Baiae was abandoned completely.

Baiae Today

However, not all of Baiae was wrecked. Over half of the city was preserved by that same volcanic action which had originally made the resort's hot springs so popular. In the late imperial period and again in the early Middle Ages, subterranean volcanic action

dropped the coastline between 6 and 10 metres (20 and 33 feet), embalming the remains of the city in underwater silt.

The city now has a new breed of tourist. Underwater archaeologists, both professional and amateur, have flocked to Baiae to delight in statues, marbles and mosaics preserved upon the seabed. Though once the protective silt has been cleared away, it requires a large-scale and ongoing effort to prevent the stonework from being colonized and destroyed by marine life.

Some statues, such as those from the nymphaeum (shrine to the nymphs) of the emperor Claudius, have been moved out of the underwater archaeological park for their own safety. These and other remnants of the Roman Las Vegas can be viewed at the nearby Parco Archeologico delle Terme di Baia without getting one's feet wet.

c. 300 BC–AD 1100
Volubilis
On the Edge of the Empire

For all its wealth and sophistication,
Volubilis was always a frontier town.

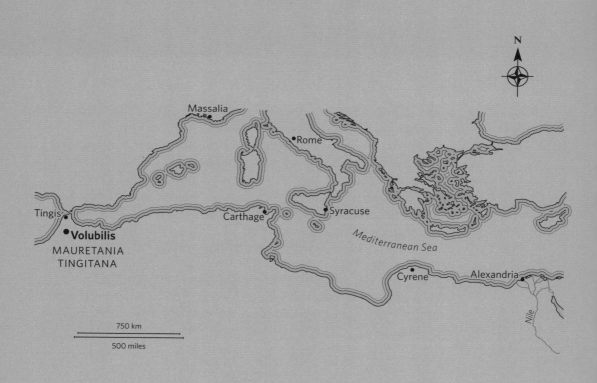

Rome's civilization spread not just across the Roman provinces but also into adjoining territories. Some places existed in a liminal space, where they were both Roman and non-Roman, part of the empire but equally influenced by the lands beyond the border. Such a city was Volubilis in North Africa.

Located in the foothills of the Rif mountains of southeastern Mauretania, Volubilis was much nearer to the Berber peoples who lived beyond the Atlas mountains than it was to the Latins of the Italian peninsula. Even though the site overlooked the fertile plain at the foot of the Jebel Zerhoun uplands, it is probable that the Romans would not have established a major city at so remote a location if there had not been a settlement there already.

Rome in Africa. Though now in ruins, the remnants of the basilica in Volubilis testify to the wealth of the lost city and the imperial reach of the Roman empire.

Beginnings

There had been a settlement of some kind at the site for thousands of years (relics have been found dating to the Neolithic era) but Volubilis formally became a city in the third century BC. Previously, it had been a trading post established by the Carthaginians for contact with the untamed Berber tribes of the interior. Among the few remains of this early period in the city's history is a temple built to the Carthaginian god Baal.

As part of the Carthaginian empire, Volubilis was indirectly affected by the Punic Wars, although the conquering legions of Scipio Africanus never ventured that far south. Instead, Volubilis became subject to Roman rule by default when Mauretania became a subject kingdom of Rome after 146 BC. Despite this, the next major influences on the cultural life of the city were not Roman but Greek.

The philhellenic Juba II, king of Mauretania (d. *c*. AD 23), was about as far from a 'barbarian' king as one could get. He was a friend of Julius Caesar and his heir Octavian, spoke Latin and Greek fluently and married Cleopatra Selene, the daughter of Cleopatra of Egypt and Mark Antony. He encouraged the arts and sciences in his kingdom, and was something of a scholar himself, publishing a treatise on Roman archaeology. Under Juba's rule Volubilis flourished to the extent that some historians believe it may have served as a second capital for his kingdom. Rich mosaics from this era have been found in the mansions of Volubilis, generally depicting themes from Greek mythology.

Roman Volubilis

After Juba's death, the Romans formally annexed his kingdom, which became the Roman province of Mauretania Tingitana. It is doubtful that the change of management greatly affected the people of Volubilis, though the protection of the legions was welcome – the Berber tribes strongly resisted attempts to push Rome's borders any further south. For all its wealth and sophistication, Volubilis was always a frontier town.

Epigraphic evidence shows that the population of the city largely consisted of Latinized Berbers, remnants of the Carthaginian population, and a small Jewish element. Nevertheless, the city was plugged directly into the mainstream Roman economic system. The plain in front of the city was ideal for growing wheat and olives, and the city of Rome had an insatiable appetite for both. Evidence for the olive industry is everywhere in Volubilis, and the remains of

Statuettes of acrobats found at Volubilis. These graceful figurines are now in the Musée Archéologique, Rabat.

olive presses are the single most common industrial artefact found in the ruins.

Another of the flourishing industries in the area was capturing and exporting exotic animals for the Roman arena. While these activities greatly benefited the merchants of Volubilis, they also constituted something of an ecological disaster, contributing directly to the extinction of the Atlas bear and the Barbary lion. The local forests were destroyed to make way for wheat and olive plantations – a process that contributed to, and was exacerbated by, the growing desertification of the region.

Peak Volubilis

Nevertheless, for the first two centuries of the imperial era Volubilis continued to thrive. Most of the city's older buildings were demolished so that newer and grander ones could be built over the remains. The city spread over an area of some 43 hectares (106 acres). A main street, the Decumanus, had broad sidewalks lined with shops (some two hundred have been identified so far) and the houses of the wealthy. At one end of the street was the imposing Arch of Caracalla (later partly rebuilt during the French colonial occupation) and at the other the so-called Tingis Gate.

Water was carried into town by an aqueduct, and from there it flowed through the city in an underground channel beneath a street running parallel to the Decumanus. Smaller mud-brick housing blocks accommodated the city's poorer citizens. Though these were often just two-room dwellings, the remains of dozens of bakeries show that the population tended to spend much of the day outdoors, including at the forum and marketplace, which occupied more than 1,000 square metres (10,750 square feet). Overall, Volubilis had a population of some twenty thousand inhabitants.

Decline

Even at its most prosperous, Volubilis was under threat from Berber tribes, and around AD 168 the administration of the emperor Marcus Aurelius ordered the construction of a 2.6-kilometre (1½-mile) circuit of defensive walls to shore up the city's somewhat *ad hoc* defences. These defences were all the more necessary as the Roman empire was plunged into crisis during the third century. During this empire-wide period of political and economic instability, Volubilis slipped out of imperial control.

A mosaic floor and Corinthian columns frame this view of the ruins of the city, looking out over the plains that were once the source of the city's agricultural wealth.

Even when a series of capable emperors later re-stabilized Roman society, Volubilis remained beyond the frontiers of Rome's shrunken borders in Africa. Now controlled by the local tribes, Volubilis seems to have remained an urban centre. From the archaeological evidence, it appears that the city's dual character allowed it to keep functioning as a Moorish city even when the Roman element lost control. The city also seems to have had a largely Christian population in this later era, which probably helped when Volubilis came briefly back under the control of the Eastern Roman empire in the sixth and seventh centuries.

By this time, Volubilis was much reduced. The collapsed economy of Italy no longer had much demand for the city's products, and an earthquake in the fifth century had created widespread devastation. After 788 the city became Islamic and for a while enjoyed a renaissance as the capital of the Muslim dynasty of the Idrisids. The ecological damage of previous centuries was catching up with the city, however, and by the eleventh century it was largely abandoned.

In the seventeenth century the ruined city was pillaged once more – this time by the Sultan of Meknes, who wanted marble columns and dressed stone to adorn his own city. More damage was wrought by a further earthquake in the eighteenth century.

Volubilis Today

Despite the centuries since its abandonment, Volubilis remains one of the best-preserved Roman cities in Africa. The dry climate has helped to preserve a treasure trove of mosaics, statuary and inscriptions. For example, archaeologists have discovered a perfectly intact bust of the younger Cato, still sitting upon its original pedestal in an abandoned room. Some of the inhabitants who fled the city in AD 285 when Roman rule collapsed never returned, leaving hoards of money and fine bronze statues buried under their houses for delighted archaeologists to unearth some 1,700 years later.

Volubilis now has a small population of researchers (since 2000, excavations have been carried out by University College London and the Moroccan Institut National des Sciences de l'Archéologie et du Patrimoine), but still almost half the city remains to be excavated. As with many a lost and rediscovered city, Volubilis is now a UNESCO World Heritage Site.

c. 700 BC–AD 790
Stabiae
Forgotten Victim of Vesuvius

The volcano buried Stabiae under some
15 metres of ash and cinders.

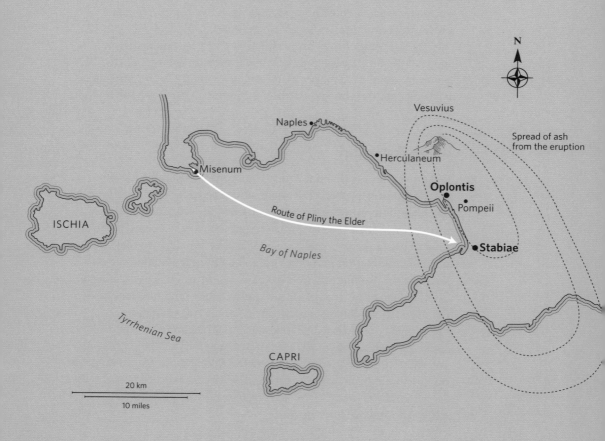

N

Vesuvius

Naples

Spread of ash
from the eruption

Herculaneum

Misenum

Oplontis

• Pompeii

ISCHIA

Route of Pliny the Elder

Bay of Naples

• **Stabiae**

Tyrrhenian Sea

CAPRI

20 km

10 miles

In the year AD 79 Mount Vesuvius erupted with catastrophic force. The volcano had been relatively quiescent for centuries and was not considered an existential threat by the locals. Indeed, the rebel gladiator Spartacus had once established a guerilla base high on the mountain slopes. Yet when Vesuvius blew, it did so in spectacular style. A column of super-heated gas pushed a cloud of ash over 30 kilometres (18½ miles) into the atmosphere, while pyroclastic surges of lava and ash rushed down the mountain slopes at the speed of an express train.

Vesuvius produced hundreds of millions of tonnes of ash and pumice in an eruption that lasted for almost a day. As is well known, the cities of Pompeii and Herculaneum were totally buried in the resultant ashfall; but so were the port city of Stabiae and the little fishing village of Oplontis.

This marble statue gives its name to the villa where it was found, the Villa del Pastore. The middle-aged shepherd carries a lamb on his shoulders, a basket of fruit and grain on one arm and a hare in the other hand.

A changing population

Stabiae was located on the coast, some 4.5 kilometres (2 miles) from Pompeii, at the eastern end of the Bay of Naples. The first evidence for occupation of the site goes back around three thousand years and the city was certainly a going concern by the eighth century BC. At this time the occupants were Etruscans, but contemporary relics from Athens, Corinth and Phoenicia testify to the cosmopolitan nature of the early settlement, which was probably a trading port.

Indeed, examination of the remains of the town's extensive necropolis suggest that the very first settlers may have been Greek merchants, who were elbowed aside by the native Etruscan population. The extensive burial site of the necropolis was in use for some four centuries, and the hundreds of tombs there allow modern researchers to map changes to the population.

After the Etruscans, it appears that Stabiae was occupied mainly by an Italic tribe from the interior called the Oscans. As a hill people, the Oscans were less interested in seafaring than in the rich agricultural hinterland of the growing city, the so-called Ager Stabianus. Consequently, merchants moved their location to nearby Pompeii, which began to eclipse Stabiae in importance. Later still the Oscans were displaced by the more warlike Samnites.

The Samnites were inveterate enemies of Rome and Stabiae joined the anti-Roman Nucerian Federation of local Samnite towns. However, recognizing that resistance was futile, Stabiae surrendered in 308 BC and the town was absorbed into Rome's growing empire. We know that the city remained loyal to Rome during the Carthaginian wars of 264–201 BC, as the heroic actions

A literal picture window from Oplontis. The Romans were fond of frescoes that purported to look out over grand architectural vistas.

of a trireme crewed by young men from Stabiae are recorded in the annals of that war. However, in the Social War of 90 BC, the city joined other Italians in the fight to force Rome to extend to them the privileges of citizenship. Instead of gaining the franchise, however, the town suffered complete destruction when the Roman legions arrived under the notoriously merciless general Cornelius Sulla. According to a text by the elder Pliny, only a single farmhouse was left standing once Sulla departed (*Natural History* 3.9.13).

Roman Stabiae

Not for the last time, Stabiae showed a remarkable talent for regeneration and within a few decades the city had re-established itself, this time as a Roman town. Roman Stabiae achieved considerable prosperity, mainly as a resort for wealthy persons who enjoyed the seaside but not the shenanigans of the fashionable crowd at Baiae. Cicero wrote to a friend that he envied him 'passing the morning hours with pleasant reading beside that large window in your room with the beautiful vista of the Bay of Stabiae before your eyes' (*Letters* 7.1.1).

The room to which Cicero refers was probably in one of the splendid mansions that lined the headland for a distance of nearly 2 kilometres (about a mile). These sat on the edge of a steep drop of almost 50 metres (164 feet) to the sea, so the views would indeed have been spectacular. Even the *villae rusticae* – those farmhouses set back from the sea in the fertile hinterland – had wealthy owners, whose farm buildings not only had threshing rooms and olive presses, but also fancy thermal baths and expensive mosaics and frescoes.

Vesuvius and the aftermath

Following pages The Villa San Marco at Stabiae. Since its discovery in the eighteenth century, this structure, one of the largest villas in the area, has been extensively restored – partly from an earthquake in 1980, which caused extensive damage to the ancient building.

The elder Pliny would have been familiar with Stabiae, because it was just along the coast from the naval base at Misenum that he commanded (in addition to being a naturalist and writer). When Vesuvius erupted, Pliny was at home with his young nephew, who later wrote letters describing the events. Inspired in part by scientific curiosity, the Plinys set off towards the eruption, but their investigation quickly became a rescue mission as they saw how many people were desperately trying to flee from the catastrophe.

Pliny (the Elder) commanded his men to head for Stabiae and evacuate as many refugees from the beach as they could. While commanding this operation Pliny collapsed and died – either from

natural causes brought on by the stress or from toxic fumes from the eruption. The volcano ultimately ejected enough material to bury most of Stabiae under some 15 metres (50 feet) of cinders – enough, as it happens, to keep the villas almost intact for millennia and the statues and frescoes in almost the same condition as when they were buried.

This was not the end of Stabiae – yet again the town struggled back to life. The first-century Roman poet Statius, in his *Silvae* (3.6),

One of many Roman imitations of the Greek sculptor Polykleitos's Doryphoros (the 'spear-carrier'). The left arm and spear are missing in action, as is the original statue, which, unlike this marble imitation from Stabiae, was cast in bronze.

In this charming fresco from Stabiae a bird alights on a shelf to investigate some fresh-plucked figs.

refers to 'vaporiferous Baiae' and 'reborn Stabiae' among the attractions of Campania. In fact, rather as with other Campanian resort towns, Stabiae only went into decline when the Roman empire itself did so. By the time that the Benedictine order of monks set up an establishment at Stabiae in the fifth century, the rest of the town was virtually abandoned, and it became totally so during the Middle Ages.

Stabiae Today

The damage done to the buildings of Stabiae by Vesuvius was compounded by the fact that the city was among the first archaeological sites to be excavated in Italy, and these eighteenth-century digs were unscientific enough to be hardly distinguishable from looting. Their main purpose was to unearth Roman artefacts, which Charles VII of Naples could bestow on his fellow monarchs as gifts.

Perhaps fortunately for Stabiae, the more spectacular remains of Pompeii were discovered soon afterwards and the ruins at Stabiae were left for a more scientific breed of archaeologists in later centuries. However, even their more careful excavation exposed the buildings to nature, and an earthquake in 1980 damaged the fragile ruins even further. Fortunately many of the valuable artefacts and paintings were by then safely stored in the museum in Naples.

A small modern village has grown up near the site, which does a thriving business catering to those well-informed tourists who know that the magnificent ruins at Stabiae offer much the same experience as a visit to nearby Pompeii, but without the crowds.

600 BC–AD 43?
Maiden Castle
Death of a Myth

Evidence of a disturbed society comes from a disproportionate number of young males whose skeletons show signs of violent death.

HADRIAN'S WALL

N

Brigantes

Lindum •

Dobunni

Iceni

Catuvellauni

Trinovantes

Cornovii

Camulodunum •

Moridunum •

Verulamium •

Silures

Londinium •

Aquae
Sulis •

Atrebates

Durotriges

• Venta Belgarum

Durnovaria

Maiden Castle
•

Dumnonii

100 km

50 miles

The story goes that at the time of the Roman invasion Britain was a largely peaceful, matriarchal society where the Druidic religion encouraged harmony with nature. Nevertheless, the Britons fought hard to repel the militaristic Romans, and one of the sites of that resistance was at the hillfort of Maiden Castle (named 'Maiden' because it was considered impregnable). Despite the Britons' heroic efforts, the superior firepower and military technology of the Romans allowed them to overwhelm the defences. They then put to the sword the men, women and children of this, one of Celtic Britain's last fortresses, which they razed to the ground.

It is an evocative and stirring tale, but sadly the only true part of it is that Maiden Castle was a hillfort. The rest is a combination of misinterpreted evidence and wishful thinking, which has obscured the real – and fascinating – story of one of Britain's most impressive Iron Age settlements.

Origins

The site of what was to become Maiden Castle sits just below the crest of a ridge on a hill some 130 metres (425 feet) above sea level near the modern city of Dorset. The hill overlooks a plain that has been occupied by humans for at least six thousand years. The first people to leave their mark on the hill did so very literally, by cutting ditches into the hillside that exposed the white chalk beneath. This mark of ownership and occupation was visible for miles, and shows that from the earliest times Maiden Castle was as much a symbol as a site. Control of the hill equated to control of the fields below, and the hill's owners were determined to make that fact clear.

An engraved fragment of a bronze plaque from the Roman era at Maiden Castle. It shows the goddess Minerva with her distinguishing spear and helmet.

Whatever the reason for this first occupation of the hilltop, it appears to have been sporadic and the effort abandoned around 5,500 years ago. In the Bronze Age, around 1000 BC, an attempt was made to farm the relatively flat hilltop, but the shallow soil was quickly exhausted. Thereafter the site was used mainly for ceremonial gatherings and burials.

The fort

At the start of the Iron Age, around 600 BC, the first hillfort appeared. It is possible that this was both an administrative centre and a refuge of last resort for the local farming population in an increasingly violent era. As time went on, the fort grew in size and importance. Its dominant position (*mai dun or* 'great hill' is a more probable

Previous pages
The massive ramparts
of the hillfort loom
over the surrounding
countryside and the
modern buildings
of Dorchester and
Martinstown.

origin of the modern name) and formidable fortifications made
the site one of the metropolises of its day.

The strong defences created a secure base for such activities
as iron smelting and trade. Most of the pottery found at the site is
imported, and the archaeological evidence shows that Maiden Castle
was one of the most important sites for the production of iron in
contemporary Britain. In fact, the settlement produced more iron
than could be sourced locally, so ore was probably imported from
Wales and the south Weald. Extensive granaries show that crops
from the plain were stored in the safety of the hillfort.

At some point the increasing population caused the somewhat
random distribution of houses to be rearranged into a more regular
street plan, though the dwellings continued to be the wattle-and-
daub roundhouses common throughout Britain at this time.

The defences

The main reason that Maiden Castle became one of the major
hillforts of Iron Age Europe was its impressive defences. These
enclosed the 19 hectares (47 acres) or so of the hilltop with multiple
ditches, combined with earth and chalk ramparts faced with timber.
Even though Maiden Castle was a major centre of iron production,
that material was still too precious to be used in the gates, which
were constructed without nails.

The weakness of the gates was partly compensated by barbicans
built to defend them, complete with pits containing impressive
numbers of slingshot stones. Such defences were clearly needed,
for contemporary hillforts elsewhere in Britain show evidence of
burning and damage consistent with violent assaults.

Further evidence of a disturbed society comes from the
disproportionate number of young males in the local cemetery.
Many of these skeletons show signs of violent death, and the
partial healing of non-lethal cuts that reached the bone testifies
to a prolonged period of warfare.

The coming of Rome

It is commonly stated that the Romans 'civilized' Britain, but when
the Romans invaded in AD 43, the Britons were fast moving in that
direction anyway. Many tribes had started issuing their own coinage,
including the Durotriges, the dominant tribe in the region of
Maiden Castle. There was extensive trade with continental Europe,
both within and outside the Roman empire. Urbanism was on the

increase in Britain, and where it was safe to do so many people had already moved from the confines of their rather cramped and inconvenient hillforts to more commodious quarters on the plain.

Under the command of the future emperor Vespasian, the Roman Legio II secured the area around Maiden Castle, and it is at this point that the heroic resistance is said to have taken place. Thirty-eight bodies of warriors have been found, all of whom died violently. There is also evidence that buildings were torched at about this time.

But ... Thirty-eight is not many burials, after a violent siege and the massacre of a settlement of a thousand people. Also, closer examination of the Roman 'catapult bolt' discovered in one of the skeletons reveals what seems to be simply a standard javelin head embedded in a morass of wishful thinking. It is significant that the dead warriors were formally buried, with proper grave goods – not something the victorious Romans would have done.

Therefore, a new picture is emerging. In this less dramatic scenario, Maiden Castle was mostly defunct and only partly occupied just before the Romans took over the area, with the former population now mainly living in the more comfortable nearby town of Durnovaria (Dorchester). The main use of Maiden Castle was as a formal burial site for Durotriges warriors who had died heroically elsewhere.

Once the *Pax Romana* was established in the area, only the east part of the fort was occupied, and that sparsely and for only a few decades more. Thereafter Maiden Castle was abandoned altogether. The surviving buildings were burned down, probably to clear the area for pasturage. Some time in the late first century AD the ditches were deliberately filled in – perhaps because a nervous Roman governor recognized that the hillfort might yet have potential as a rebel stronghold.

In the fourth century a Romano-Celtic temple was built on the hill, but it was allowed to fall into disrepair. After this, the population of Maiden Castle was almost exclusively sheep and the occasional cow.

Maiden Castle Today

In its prime Maiden Castle was the premier hillfort in the British Isles, and as such is well worth a visit. Indeed, so many people have visited the site since it was properly excavated in the 1930s that English Heritage have taken the location under their protection. There is now better organization for visitors, with parking facilities and information boards posted at strategic locations. The site is open all year round.

Timgad
The City of Trajan

When an explorer claimed to have discovered a complete
Roman city in Algeria, few believed him.

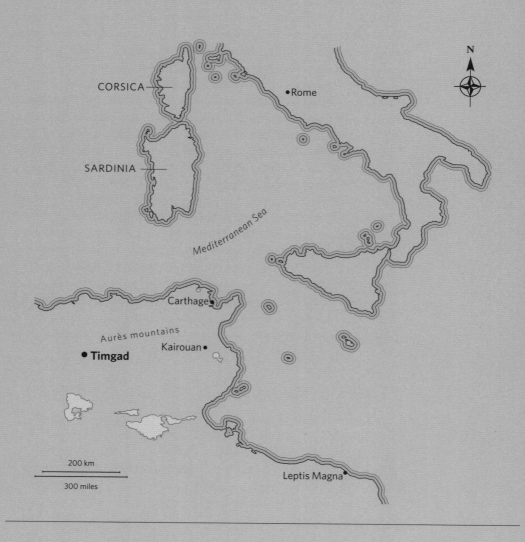

CORSICA

• Rome

SARDINIA

Mediterranean Sea

Carthage •

Aurès mountains

• **Timgad**   Kairouan •

N

200 km

300 miles

Leptis Magna •

Creating a city from scratch is a risky and highly expensive exercise, even when undertaken by a great and powerful ruler. Of all the dozens of cities founded by Alexander the Great, only his eponymous creation in Egypt has survived as a great city. The pages of this book are littered with failed cities launched by ambitious rulers, such as the Tigranocerta of Tigranes of Armenia and the vanity projects of the Egyptian pharaohs. Why, then, should Trajan, one of Rome's most level-headed emperors, decide to create a city in what is now the Algerian desert, hundreds of kilometres from anywhere?

A city from nothing

One reason was that, at the time of Timgad's founding in AD 100, the Sahara had not reached its present extent. Trajan's new city stood, not on a desiccated plateau, but on fertile land, some 770 kilometres (480 miles) southeast of the modern city of Algiers. In fact, one reason for the choice of location was precisely because there were no major cities nearby. Trajan felt that a substantial settlement would awe and intimidate the hostile Berber tribesmen in the nearby Aurès mountains (part of the Atlas range) and impress them with the superiority of Roman civilization. Even if the city

A view of the ruins of Timgad, looking towards the Arch of Trajan, with the Aurès mountains in the background.

Detail of a mosaic from Timgad depicting the Titan Tethys, wife of Oceanus. This mosaic is part of a splendid collection in the Archaeological Museum of Timgad in Algeria.

failed to do its job as a cultural icon, it could help militarily by supporting the Roman army's Legio III Augusta, which was based at Lambaesis, 17 kilometres (10½ miles) away.

In fact, the kernel of the city may have been the original base of the Third Legion. The new civilian population of Timgad was really only semi-civilian to start with, as Trajan intended the city's inhabitants to be largely retired soldiers and their families – a sort of military reserve that could be called up in an emergency.

Careful design

The new city was called, less than snappily, Colonia Marciana Traiana Thamugadi. 'Colonia' because its inhabitants were Roman citizens, 'Marciana' because 'Marcia' was a common name in Trajan's family, and 'Traiana' because even Trajan had some personal vanity. 'Thamugadi' is a word of apparently Berber origin, but of uncertain meaning.

The inhabitants of this verbosely named city would have immediately found the layout of their new home familiar. The town's designers had the advantage of starting from scratch, and their chosen street layout strongly resembled the design of a Roman army camp. The major roads were oriented along two axes – the Cardo, an avenue running from north to south, and the Decumanus Maximus, which went from east to west. These streets, like others in the city, were paved with limestone flagstones which still protect the surface some two millennia later.

All streets ran parallel to one or other of these main thoroughfares, dividing the city into an orthogonal grid. All intersections were right angles. The main difference from a military camp was that the Cardo did not run right across the settlement, but stopped at the intersection with the Decumanus. At this point, several city blocks were sacrificed to create a substantial forum at the heart of the city. This forum was where candidates for election gave speeches and where imperial officials sat in judgment in court cases. Citizens came to the offices there to deal with the city administration, and also to socialize and shop, because the stalls in the forum constituted the city's major market venue.

A rising city

Again, building from scratch meant that water pipes and sewers could be laid in a rational manner, and the abundance of water at that time meant that the city was blessed with an unusually high number of *thermae* – public baths. There were four major baths and many more minor ones. These were built to the high standards of the best Roman architecture. In fact, a set of similar Roman baths at nearby Hammam Essalihine is still in use today.

The town planners intended the city to be a deliberate statement of Roman culture, so the buildings were built on a grand scale. Indeed, the scale was somewhat grander than necessary because the builders were compensating for being forced to use mostly local stone rather than more impressive marble – which had to be imported over a considerable distance. A triumphal arch and a temple to Capitoline Jupiter dominated the city centre, and the city boasted a substantial library. Around AD 160 cultural life was further enhanced by a theatre, seating over 3,500 people, which was carved into a hillside just outside the city.

By that time Timgad's population had outgrown the originally planned ten thousand citizens and some of the new settlers made their homes outside the walls. (Though walled, Timgad was never strongly fortified.) Archaeological evidence shows that, as well as the original Roman element, the city now had also a distinct Numidian and particularly Berber population.

Decline and fall

The city was a thriving nexus of Roman civilization for the next 250 years, but by the fourth century was in mild decline, partly due to a changing climate and partly because the entire Roman empire was becoming somewhat dilapidated. At the end of the century the city – now Christian – was wracked with religious controversy as the diocese took what turned out to be the wrong side in what is now called the Donatist Schism.

A century later a migrant Vandal tribe – Arian Christians – resolved the religious debate once and for all by taking and comprehensively pillaging Timgad, sending the city into terminal decline. Recalcitrant Berber tribesmen from the Aurès mountains then finished off what the Vandals had left. When soldiers of the Eastern Roman empire arrived in the sixth century they found the city deserted. They built a large fort nearby, and the city had a ghost population until the Arab conquest, after which Timgad was finally abandoned.

Timgad Today

So thoroughly was Timgad lost that when a Scottish explorer of the eighteenth century claimed to have found a complete Roman city abandoned in the wilds of Algeria, few people believed him.

It was only after the French occupation of Algeria that systematic archaeological work began. (Some of the damage done by those early, misguided efforts has yet to be undone.) Because Timgad was unoccupied after its fall, there were no later buildings to interfere with excavations and the city was quickly revealed to be an exemplary demonstration of Roman town planning.

As well as early archaeological efforts (which did preserve some fine mosaics from the town houses of the wealthy), further damage was done to Timgad in the past century by – ironically – a festival of music and culture. This international jamboree has been held at Timgad since the 1960s, with festivalgoers adding graffiti and rubbish to the site and technicians disfiguring the theatre with pipes and cables.

Timgad has been a World Heritage Site since 1982. Aware of the damage to both the ancient city and the nation's cultural reputation, the local authorities now stage the festival at a modern faux-Roman theatre situated a safe distance from the Roman ruins.

Trajan's arch in Timgad, shown here, is a larger structure than the emperor's better-known arch in Beneventum, and is one of several monumental structures that Trajan left scattered across the empire.

AD 130–*c.* 950
Antinopolis
City of the Drowned God

A city founded to celebrate the apotheosis of the emperor Hadrian's lover into a god.

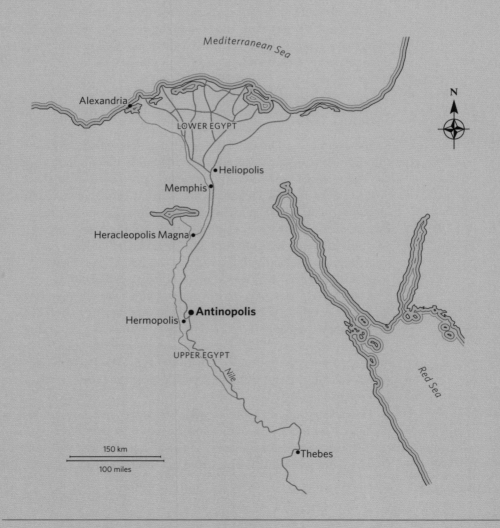

In the year AD 123, the emperor Hadrian was introduced to a beautiful youth from the province of Bithynia in Asia Minor. Antinous was around 12 years old, and it is generally believed that the emperor immediately entered into a sexual relationship with the boy. By contemporary standards this was quite acceptable, and those at the imperial court became accustomed to Antinous as the emperor's companion, even as Hadrian toured the provinces of the Roman empire.

The couple were inseparable for the next six years or so, after which their relationship became more problematic. In a mirror image of modern morality, Roman public opinion tolerated Hadrian's relationship with an underage teenager, but the emperor having a homosexual relationship with a full-grown male was less acceptable.

The problem resolved itself while Hadrian was on a tour of Egypt in AD 130. While the imperial party was travelling up the Nile, Antinous drowned in mysterious circumstances. Was he murdered by courtiers desperate to avoid a public relations disaster? Did the emperor kill him during a lover's tiff? Or – the most probable theory – did Antinous, distraught at the problems he was causing his beloved, decide to sacrifice himself?

It is significant that Antinous died at one of the most religiously symbolic points along the river. This was at the city of Hermopolis, sacred to the Egyptian deity Thoth, god of magic, healing and

Portrait bust of Antinous, created after his deification. The figure wears the *nemes*-headcloth, a type of headgear worn by Egyptian royalty.

arcane wisdom. As the priests explained to the distraught Hadrian afterwards, anyone who drowned under such circumstances was certain to be incorporated into the being of the god Osiris.

Founding Antinopolis

If that were so, decreed Hadrian, then a city would be founded right then and there, on the opposite bank of the Nile to Hermopolis, to celebrate the apotheosis of the emperor's boy-lover into a god. The city was to be named Antinopolis to celebrate his memory, and designed as one giant memorial. A keen student of city planning and architecture, Hadrian subsumed his grief into the layout of this new foundation.

The site of the city was already occupied by the village of Hir-we, which had been there since at least the time of the Egyptian New Kingdom (*c.* 1550–1069 BC). This village Hadrian razed to the ground, sparing only a temple of Ramesses II and a cult centre of the benevolent god Bes. (Bes was a household protector whose divine portfolio included killing snakes, fighting off malign influences and protecting children.)

Cynics have noted that the death of Antinous provided an awfully convenient excuse for the Romans to establish a significant outpost of Greco-Roman culture near the imperial frontier. In fact, the city would be more Hellenic than Roman, both because Hadrian was a noted philhellene, and because settlements in the eastern part of the empire tended to be more Greco than Roman.

Greeks were encouraged to emigrate to the new city, and given special privileges for doing so. All settlers were given Roman citizenship, and if they married Egyptian women their offspring automatically gained the same privileges. Indeed, papyrus fragments recovered from the region often make references to a 'Citizen of Antinopolis', afforded special treatment because of that status.

A Greek city in central Egypt

One of the central features of the new city was (naturally) a mausoleum of Antinous, and statues of the boy-god lined the streets. These streets were broad, paved and lined with shops interspersed with elegant colonnades. The city had a rudimentary wall of some 5.5 kilometres (3½ miles) in length. This wall was more for administrative purposes than defence and the side of the city on the banks of the Nile remained open. The main colonnade ran the length of the city, linking the theatre at one end with the mausoleum at the other.

Detail from a cloth found in a woman's tomb in Antinopolis, known as 'Sabrina's shawl'. It holds a number of richly coloured scenes from myth, such as this representation of Bellerophon trampling upon the Chimera.

The city probably had a bustling harbour, for the location was convenient for goods arriving from India and China. These were carried from the Red Sea port of Berenice, along the newly built Via Hadriana, to Antinopolis and then shipped down the Nile. Outside the walls stood a massive hippodrome, while within the walls were numerous temples, a theatre and a triumphal arch.

To further ensure that Antinous would never be forgotten, Hadrian also instituted an annual festival known as the Antinoeia. This featured athletic tournaments, equestrian events and cultural celebrations such as musical competitions and theatrical performances. The rich prizes attracted top talent from all over Egypt and beyond, and for centuries the Antinoeia was one of the major events in central Egypt.

'Mummy portraits' from the second century AD could be almost photorealistic. From this picture painted on linden wood, one can easily imagine how this citizen of the city looked when alive.

Painted head of a woman from Antinopolis wearing a series of necklaces.

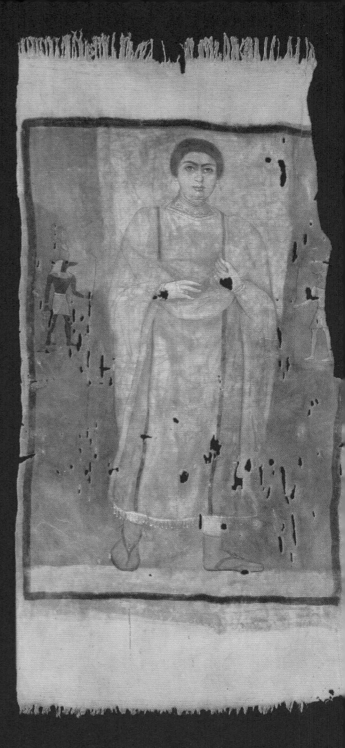

A woman wearing a fringed tunic prepares to step from a doorway flanked by Egyptian gods in this shroud from Antinopolis.

Later Antinopolis

One of the most famous later citizens of Antinopolis was the fourth-century mathematician, Serenus, who devised a technique for calculating the geometry of a cylinder. St Colluthus, a Christian, was famed for his martyrdom in either 304 or 308. (The anti-Christian purges of the emperor Diocletian were particularly ferocious in the city.) Despite Diocletian's best efforts, Antinopolis was Christian by the fifth century, when one traveller reported there were at least twelve 'monasteries for women' in the city, as well as numerous anchorites and holy men living outside the walls. The city was the seat of not one but two bishops.

By that time, the city's origins had become something of an embarrassment to its citizens, and some texts refer to the city as 'Antinoe'. In the Byzantine era the name change was made official and the city became Ansena.

Ansena/Antinoe/Antinopolis survived the Muslim conquest of Egypt in 641 and features in written records in the 900s. However, by then the city was already in decline and it slipped from the historical record thereafter.

Antinopolis Today

The next time anyone paid attention to the lost city was at the turn of the nineteenth century, when Napoleon of France made an attempt to conquer Egypt. He brought with him scholars and surveyors, who examined the site of Antinopolis and noted the remains of the temples and colonnades. They also recorded that much of the city's stone had vanished to become part of the walls of homes and mosques in nearby towns and villages, especially al-Sheikh Ibada, which stands today beside the site.

Visitors to Antinopolis will find almost none of the remains described by the Napoleonic surveyors. The site was almost completely destroyed by industrialists of the early modern era, who pillaged the limestone blocks to burn for lime and dismantled other ancient buildings for stone to reuse in a local dam.

The best option for those wanting to examine ancient Antinopolis is to go to nearby el-Rodah, where many of the ancient structures have been rebuilt as a modern sugar factory. At the actual site of the city, apart from a few desolate remnants of the ancient hippodrome, the rest of Antinopolis is truly lost.

PART FOUR
The Empire's Edge and Beyond

In the last years of the Roman empire, the Mediterranean world suddenly rediscovered the importance of walls. Even mighty Rome itself, which for centuries had sprawled undefended into the surrounding countryside, had to be hastily girded with fortifications by the emperor Aurelian. The fifth century AD has been called 'The Age of Migrations', and many of the barbarian hordes arriving in Western Europe possessed little more than swords and a fine disregard for property rights.

Many once-thriving cities failed to make it into the medieval era in the face of this onslaught, either because they were undefended, or indefensible. Others faded away because the trade routes upon which they depended ceased to exist. Few new cities were founded, and older ones shrank dramatically. Between AD 350 and 650 the population of Rome is estimated to have fallen from 1,100,000 to 30,000 inhabitants. Other cities were simply abandoned altogether.

In some parts of the empire cities had been shrinking even before barbarian invasions abruptly reduced the population. The West was in demographic decline, and such economic growth as did occur largely took place in the country. The so-called 'villa economy' created self-sufficient units centred about the villa of a local landowner. (This system survived the fall of the Roman empire – in fact, the boundaries of such economic units are often reflected in, for example, the borders of the modern English parish. Surnames such as 'Schumaker' [cobbler], 'Molinaro' [miller] and 'Thatcher' reflect the roles of people within communities.)

From the Forum to the Cathedral

Within those cities that endured, life changed to adapt to new social and economic circumstances. Theatres and bathhouses did not fit with the new Christian ethos, and mostly fell into disrepair, while much greater emphasis was placed upon the spiritual. The cathedral replaced the forum as the focal point of many cities, and some of the greatest urban architecture of the age is manifested in those superb buildings, which often took centuries to complete. The citadel or castle assumed a new and much greater importance.

In this later era, rather than being created by administrative fiat, new settlements grew organically, sometimes around army camps (consider cities such as Lancaster or Frankfurt). Some names reflect the reason why the cities developed, for example, at river crossings such as at Oxford or Innsbruck. Everywhere, uninhabited cities found a new role as quarries for dressed stone that could be reused elsewhere. (Anyone who wants to see the buildings of the Roman forum is advised to go to the Vatican, where the masonry of those ancient edifices has been redistributed into St Peter's Basilica.) What remained of the derelict cities was a source of melancholic wonder for later generations, as is demonstated by this passage from the Old English poem 'The Ruin', by an unknown author:

Wondrous is the masonry, broken by fate

Smashed town houses, the decaying labour of giants

Fallen the roofs, ruined the towers

The gate is frozen, hoarfrost on lime

Undermined by old age

The chipped rooftops collapse

Dead and gone the mighty builders

Taken into the grasp of the earth.

A hundred generations have passed

While this rust-stained lichen-grey
wall has stood

Reign after reign through all the storms.

The high, wide gate is down

But the stones remain.

Yet the death of the Roman city was not the death of the city itself. Across Europe, as populations grew, the cities revived. In the east, under the Muslim caliphs, the cities had never gone away. At about the same time that 'The Ruin' was written, Baghdad was founded and in later centuries went on to become one of the greatest cities in the world. Nevertheless, in places such as Beta Samati in East Africa and Derinkuyu in Anatolia, cities were still built and later forgotten.

The impetus that had brought humans into cities in the first place was never lost, and the cities of later medieval Europe were busy, brawling (and profoundly unhygienic) places. It was here that the seeds of the Renaissance were planted, and the early modern era began – inspired, at least in part, by those haunting reminders of antiquity that still littered the landscape.

Before 1000 BC–AD 1400
Palmyra
City of the Desert Queen

Famed for its beautiful location, its rich soil and the abundance of its sweet water.

Pliny the Elder

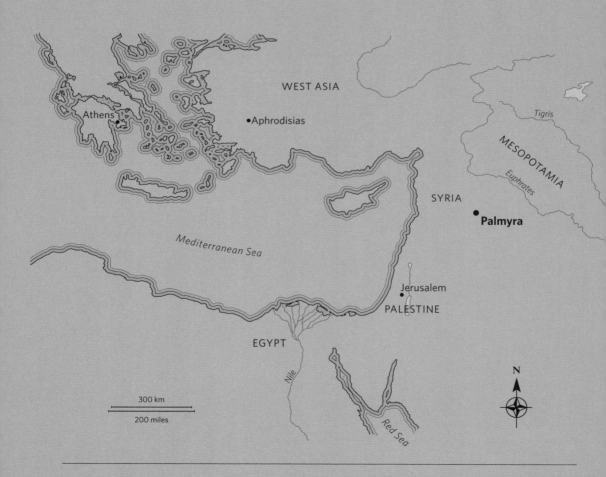

U rban life has a long history in the area around the ancient city of Palmyra. Damascus, 215 kilometres (135 miles) to the southwest, is probably the oldest continuously inhabited place on Earth, where the first settlers arrived some ten thousand years ago. Though now abandoned, Palmyra is not far behind, with the first traces of human occupation at the Efqa spring site dating back to around 7000 BC.

An oasis settlement

It is uncertain at what time humans settled permanently at the complex of interlocking oases which was to later become Palmyra – or Tadmor, to give the city the name used by its inhabitants. Most of these oases were fed by springs originating at the Wadi al-Qubur, which became the main nexus of settlement. (*Al-Qubur* simply means 'riverbed'.) However, by 1000 BC, Palmyra/Tadmor was an established city, and the newcomers joined the Aramaean population already in residence.

The multicultural population added Hebrews to the mix around 950 BC, when the city fell into the orbit of the kingdom of Solomon, who, the Bible says, 'built Tadmor in the wilderness' (2 Chronicles 8.4). Clay tablets from the Mesopotamian city of Mari also mention the

Funerary head of a woman from Palmyra. Dating from the third century AD, this limestone sculpture shows Roman influences in style, while the headdress is distinctly native to the region.

city as a trading centre, a role which Palmyra was to keep over the coming millennia.

The principal building of the city was the temple of the god Bel (the name being a derivative of Baal, who was widely worshipped in the region). Excavations around and beneath the temple clearly show the timeline of settlement.

A temple in time

These excavations take us back in time from the somewhat makeshift constructions of the early modern era, to buildings from the Arab caliphate, and back to the Byzantine empire. Late Roman artefacts have been found, and many from the third century AD when the city was in its prime. The temple of Bel itself was somewhat earlier, being built in AD 32 while Tiberius was emperor of Rome.

Beneath this there is a layer marking a period of Hellenistic culture associated with the Seleucid empire of Alexander the Great's heirs, and artefacts showing that at one point the city was either occupied by, or traded extensively with, the Assyrians. Other tools found here go back to the early Bronze Age, and the earliest ones date from the Stone Age around 7000 BC.

For most of its life Palmyra was a way-station for caravans crossing the Syrian desert. While it fell under the aegis of different empires at different times, the city itself was isolated enough to retain a large degree of autonomy. In fact, there seems to have been little need for walls until the first century BC when, in an attempt to make the city defensible, fortifications were built to cover those points where the surrounding hills did not do the job naturally. These walls failed to hold off the expanding Roman empire, and Palmyra became Roman in 64 BC.

Roman Palmyra

It was about this time that Tadmor became Palmyra to westerners. Both names (the Latin and the native Palmyrean Aramaic) come from one of the major exports of the city – dates, from its abundant palms, of which Palmyra boasted several dozen varieties. By whatever name, the city flourished under Roman rule and grew from a layover stop for desert caravans to a major trading centre in its own right. Partly this was due to the prosperity brought to the region by the *Pax Romana*, and partly to Palmyra's position between the Romans and the Parthian empire to the east.

In his *Natural History*, written in the early first century AD, the Roman writer Pliny the Elder reports (5.21.25):

> The city of Palmyra is famed for its beautiful location, its rich soil and the abundance of its sweet water. The sands of the desert surround the fields on all sides, so that nature itself separates the city from the rest of the world. Its location between the empires of Rome and Parthia give it some degree of independence, because when international tensions run high both empires never fail to give the city their careful attention.

In Palmyra, traders exchanged goods from both civilizations. Slaves, thoroughbred horses, olive oil and exotic spices were sold in the main square, along with silk, jade and tortoiseshell imported along the Silk Road from China. This square was called the agora after the Hellenic style, but archaeology shows that it operated more in the manner of an eastern *souk*.

E pluribus unum

In fact Palmyra never became either Greek, Roman or Persian but remained a fusion of all these cultures, with a strong native tradition mixed in. Greek, rather than Latin, was used for commercial purposes, and among themselves the people spoke a unique dialect of Aramaean. Like the populace that worshipped them, the city's gods were mainly Semitic in origin, with additions to the pantheon imported from Mesopotamia and the south.

As well as the Temple of Bel, other temples were dedicated to the gods Nabu, Al-lat and Baal Hammon. The priests were mainly drawn from the leading clans who made up the hereditary government of Palmyra. It is not known how many clans there were, but modern research has identified at least thirty. The aristocratic dead were sometimes mummified after the Egyptian tradition, and buried in distinctive tower-style family mausoleums in the city's extensive necropolis.

Rebel state

As the Roman empire declined in the third century AD, the fortunes of Palmyra rose. A man called Odaenathus made himself ruler of the city in the 250s. Odaenathus tried by diplomacy to secure Palmyra's trading position with the Persians, and when that failed he turned to military force. Palmyra switched from being a trading centre to a military power, and in that role the Palmyrenes not only defeated the Persians but brought much of the Roman east under their sway.

Odaenathus himself died abruptly in 267, and the main beneficiary of his somewhat suspicious death was his wife Zenobia. Ruling as regent for the youthful son of the late king, Zenobia expanded Palmyra's power into Anatolia and Egypt. This brought Zenobia into conflict with the Romans, who had for centuries regarded these lands as their own. Unfortunately for Palmyra, Rome was under the command of the highly competent emperor Aurelian, and his Roman legions easily outmatched Palmyra's archers and camel cavalry.

At first Aurelian was careful to preserve Palmyra, which he valued as an economic hub, but a later rebellion caused him to lose his temper (Aurelian was famously irascible). The second Roman occupation of Palmyra saw the city looted and razed to the ground and it never really recovered from the devastation. The population dropped from an estimated 200,000 to around a tenth of that number.

Later Palmyra

A Roman-style bas-relief believed to be from Palmyra showing aristocrats in Parthian clothing ahead of riders on camels.

There are signs that Palmyra now became a Roman military base, with the town's economic activity based upon supporting the garrison. The later emperor Diocletian attempted to restore the city, but without much success. By the Byzantine era it was little more than a regional administrative centre, although there was something of a revival under the Arab Umayyad caliphate.

In the 1400s warriors of the Mongol warlord Timur (also known as Tamerlane) swept through Palmyra and massacred the inhabitants. Later still, a tiny village was established within the ruins of the Temple of Bel. In the 1930s the French colonial rulers of the area moved these last occupants of the once-great city out to a new purpose-built village so that they could properly excavate the ruins.

Palmyra Today

In the first quarter of the twenty-first century, Palmyra made news as the victim of yet another wave of invaders. These were the fanatics of the so-called Islamic State, who, in 2015, blew up some of the city's surviving temples. Since the recapture of the city in 2017 some of the damage has been restored, and a concerted international effort has reconstructed a three-dimensional model of part of the destroyed city from existing films, photographs and archaeological records.

Palmyra has been a UNESCO World Heritage Site since 1980, though it remains unsafe for tourists at the time of writing. Nevertheless, in 2016, as a sign of better times to come, the Mariinsky Orchestra of St Petersburg gave a concert performance in Palmyra to an audience of international dignitaries.

Limestone sculpture from Palmyra depicting a woman of the third century AD in native dress with necklaces and other jewelry.

4 BC–AD 9
Waldgirmes
The Roman Germany That Might Have Been

Gone after just five years, and so comprehensively that no-one today knows its original name.

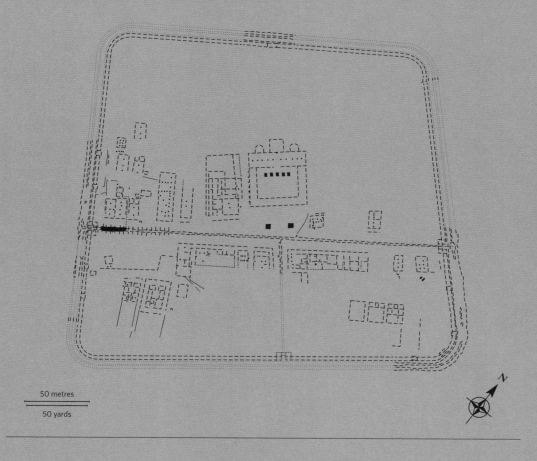

50 metres

50 yards

N

Silver brooch from Waldgirmes, measuring 3 centimetres (1 inch) across. Recovered from where it was once lost in a ditch alongside the settlement, it is one of the few finds dated to the time of first occupation of the site.

As the first century AD began, the Roman conquest of Germany was going smoothly. Rome's legions had reached the River Elbe in Central Europe, which seemed a natural eastern boundary for what the emperor Augustus reckoned would make a tidy new imperial province.

Roman legionaries arrived in the Lahn Valley, a region of thick forest and low rolling hills some 100 kilometres (62 miles) east of the Rhine. They chose a highly defensible location beside the river and set up temporary barracks, though their intention was not to conquer, but to build a city.

Perhaps this was intended as a *colonia* (a military outpost to secure territory), or a settlement for retired veterans. Or perhaps – as the ambitious layout of the town suggests – it was to be a centre for provincial administration, where local tribesmen and Roman settlers and merchants could work together. As the historian Cassius Dio remarked, at this time 'The barbarians were adapting to Roman ways, were learning to hold markets, and meet in peaceful gatherings' (*Roman History* 56.18).

Today, the permanent settlement is clearly distinguishable from the temporary work camp. The early town buildings have stone foundations, with proper sewers and lead-lined water pipes. The work camp had less permanent foundations, lightly used refuse pits and earth latrines.

Civitas ab initio (a city from scratch)

Because the city was a completely new foundation, the legionaries could set to work with characteristic military precision. A wooden wall some 3.5 metres (12 feet) high was built to protect the new settlement, if necessary, until help could arrive from the legionary base at Dorlar. This wall enclosed the 8 hectares (20 acres) of the main town and had three gates, located on the east, west and south sides. A road ran straight across the settlement from east to west. So neatly was everything laid out that the first modern archaeologists to visit the site immediately assumed that they were looking at a Roman army encampment.

However, this was no army base. There was no barracks building and very little military kit has been found. Instead, this was the nucleus about which the Romans expected a serious city to grow. In the middle was a large forum with a standard Roman basilica beside it. One of the first things the new citizens did was to erect an imposing statue in the middle of the forum, depicting a man on horseback.

The subject was probably the emperor Augustus, for the statue demonstrated serious commitment. For a start, the limestone for the pediment was imported from Gaul, probably along the River Lahr (which allowed easy access to the Roman world, including the major Roman base of Castra Vetera on the lower Rhine). The statue itself weighed hundreds of kilograms, and seems to have been plated in gold leaf, all the better to overawe the natives who joined the Romans in making the new settlement their home.

The ethnic make-up of the town is a fascinating combination of Roman and Germanic. The civic buildings were unmistakably Roman, though their part-timber construction shows that it was intended that they would be replaced by more imposing structures in the future. Nevertheless, the stone part of the construction makes these the oldest Roman masonry buildings found in Germania. Yet while the proto-city had all the hallmarks of a classic Roman town, with some Roman-style homes, other residential buildings were of German longhouse construction. This suggests that there was a mixed population in the city from the start.

Some Romans set up workshops and kilns and began to turn out pottery in their distinctive style, but other pots found at the site were distinctly Germanic. It seems the locals preferred to use their traditional ceramics rather than imports from Gaul or other Roman towns north of the Alps. About 20 per cent of the ceramics used at Waldgirmes were of hand-made native design.

The end

With workshops, smithies and potteries, an administrative centre and a marketplace in the forum, where farmers could sell produce from the fertile local fields, Waldgirmes was a fully functioning city within a year or two of the legionaries first breaking ground. Then, less than a decade after the new city was established, everything went horribly wrong.

Almost certainly, the disaster that struck Waldgirmes was related to an even greater disaster that struck the Roman legions further south in the Teutoburg Forest at Kalkriese. In AD 9, three Roman legions, the entire Roman garrison of Germania, were ambushed while moving into winter quarters and wiped out, as part of a nationalist rebellion that would ultimately end the Roman occupation. Soon after, the Roman settlement at Waldgirmes came to a violent end. We do not know if the Romans pulled out of the town and destroyed it behind them, or if the local tribesmen did the job for them.

How to lose a province. This 1873 painting by German historical painter Peter Janssen shows the moment when the Roman legions were overwhelmed in a German ambush. Thereafter Roman occupation of Germany, including Waldgirmes, came to an end.

The defensive wall was completely burned down, and the imposing equestrian statue shattered into thousands of pieces. The largest surviving piece, the horse's head, was tossed into the well, where it was sheltered through the centuries by two millstones that were thrown in after it. These millstones were almost completely new, and had recently been imported from settlements to the northwest. Other debris, including tools and buckets, was also tossed into the well, where items were so well preserved that they can be dated exactly – the most recent being a ladder made from wood cut in the autumn of AD 9.

Nothing suggests that the Romans remained long after AD 9 and the only other evidence of Roman occupation at the site is a temporary marching camp established by the army, possibly during the ferocious retaliatory campaigns that the Romans launched to avenge the loss of the province. Yet their planned regional centre was gone, and so comprehensively that even today no-one knows its name.

Waldgirmes Today

The ancient Roman settlement is now called Waldgirmes, after the nearby village. The residents noticed that Roman pottery sherds kept turning up in a local field, and in 1993 archaeologists came to investigate.

Ground-penetrating radar showed geometrically laid out streets, so the site was assumed to be a military camp until it slowly became clear that this was something altogether more exciting. Until then it had been assumed that Dio's claim that 'new cities were founded' (56.18) in Germania was a rhetorical device to show how peaceful the region had become, rather than a literal fact.

That a town could be founded without a military base in the immediate vicinity has caused historians to rethink the political situation in Germania before the nationalist rebellion. Evidently Romanization was more advanced than previously believed. This leaves open the tantalizing question of whether, if Rome's garrison had not perished in that one devastating ambush at Kalkriese, Germania could indeed have eventually become a Roman province alongside Gaul.

The legionaries are back in Waldgirmes today, as re-enactors for a lively tourist scene that includes gladiators, a reconstructed hypocaust and a dedicated visitor centre. Many of the finds from the site are on display in the local Heimatmuseum, but visitors must travel to the Archaeological Museum of Frankfurt am Main to see the rest.

Glass intaglio from Waldgirmes, possibly depicting Niobe, a tragic figure from Greek myth.

AD 50–106
Sarmizegetusa Regia
Dacian Stronghold

A planned city designed to be the religious,
political and economic centre of a new nation.

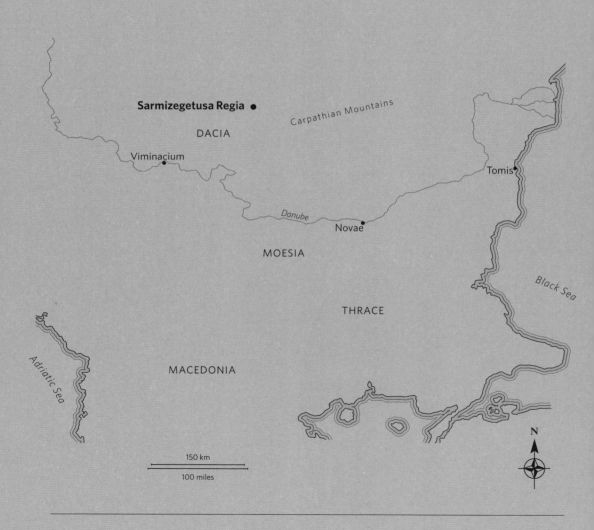

Sarmizegetusa Regia •

DACIA

Carpathian Mountains

Viminacium •

Tomis •

Danube

Novae •

MOESIA

Black Sea

THRACE

Adriatic Sea

MACEDONIA

N

150 km

100 miles

The Dacians were a Thracian people – tall, with reddish hair and blue eyes – whose warriors had terrorized the folk of northern Greece for centuries. In the modern era there is a tendency to divide the ancient world into 'civilized' folk (such as the Greeks, Egyptians and Romans) and 'barbarians'. It is assumed that the civilized peoples were busily building baths and theatres, while the barbarians were still picking lice out of their beards.

This is a misconception. The swirl of knowledge that spread around the Mediterranean world after 800 BC spread to all the peoples of the region, but some were slower to adopt all aspects of this knowledge. The Thracians were world-class metalworkers, but disinclined to urban life. The city of Sarmizegetusa Regia, however, shows what these 'barbarian' people could do if they wished.

Origins

The ancient state of Dacia was largely created by the efforts of one king, Burebista. The start of this king's reign is uncertain, but it lasted several decades, until his death in 44 BC. Burebista's great achievement was to unite the warring tribes of Dacia into a single nation, which occupied much of what is today Transylvania in central Romania.

A new nation required a new capital, since Burebista's previous capital – most probably a place called Argedava – was too closely linked with his own Geto-Dacian tribal group. A site was chosen in the Carpathian mountains. Defence was a top priority: access to the capital was controlled by a complex of six fortresses (each of which

A Medusa head from the Temple of Aesculapius in Ulpia Traiana Sarmizegetusa, second or third century AD.

is now a valued archaeological site in its own right). Sarmizegetusa Regia itself was erected on a southerly ridge near the top of Mount Muncelu, some 1,200 metres (3,950 feet) above sea level.

From the beginning, Sarmizegetusa Regia was designed to be the religious, political and economic centre of the new nation, as well as its best-defended stronghold. Its design and construction equalled those of any new city within Rome's empire, not least because it was partly built by former Roman subjects. Dacian warriors kidnapped Greco-Roman craftsmen from northern Greece and towns along the Danube, and probably hired others. The result was a city featuring the latest concepts in civil and military architecture, with municipal plumbing and sewage systems built in from the start.

Designer city

Sarmizegetusa Regia seems to have had four separate areas of urban function, in two locations. The administrative area was closely linked with a temple complex near the eastern gate, today called the Sacred Area. This, in turn, was close to the main citadel of the city, altogether covering an area of 3 hectares (7½ acres). Further downhill, on a series of artificial terraces, was a more general residential area, which was partly combined with the city's manufacturing district (ancient craftsmen tended to live above the shop). In this area, water was piped directly to the homes of some of the wealthier citizens. Overall, the average citizen of Sarmizegetusa Regia appears to have been as comfortable as any denizen of Athens or Rome, and enjoyed many of the same amenities.

The chief Dacian god was Zalmoxis, whose chief priest was apparently a person of importance in the city. The remains of some seven temples have been found, along with a large altar. While the details of Dacian religious worship are still unclear, there are evident syncretic links with the Greco-Roman gods Mercury, Venus and (naturally) Mars. One of the more enigmatic structures in the Sacred Area is the so-called Andesite Sun, a 7-metre (23-foot) circle named for the type of stone from which it is constructed. It is uncertain what this enigmatic pavement represented, but radii, extending from the centre, point towards the major structures of the city, and one points due north. (The solar disc was a common Dacian symbol.)

One reason for the location of Sarmizegetusa Regia was that the dense forests of the Carpathians, combined with abundant reserves of iron ore, made the mountain stronghold an ideal site for metalworking, a craft at which the Dacians excelled. Hundreds of metal artefacts have been excavated from the industrial area of

The enigmatic timber posts of the so-called circular sanctuary in the Sacred Area of Sarmizegetusa Regia. Despite the name, the purpose of this odd construction remains unknown.

the city: specialized tools for craftsmen and farmers and a vast array of weaponry, ranging from knives to the distinctive Dacian pole-axe, called the falx. (The latter weapon so worried the Roman legions that they made special adaptations to their armour to counter it.)

War with Rome

United Dacia was certainly not a peaceful Dacia. The social structure of the nation was predicated on warfare, and the warrior culture of the Dacians found a ready outlet in the farms and townships of the Roman empire, which was expanding right to Dacia's borders. The new Roman province of Pannonia, in particular, suffered repeated devastation from Dacian raids in the late first century AD. The emperor Domitian tried to contain the attacks, but his own weak political position meant that he was unwilling either to leave Rome himself, or to entrust a large army to anyone else. In the end Domitian resorted to bribing the Dacians to keep the peace.

A more decisive Roman solution to the problem of Dacian aggression had to wait for political stability under the emperor Trajan (r. AD 98–117). After perfunctory negotiations with the Dacian king Decebalus, Trajan decided on direct military action. As was often the

Roman strategy, this involved pointing the legions at something the enemy valued – in this case Sarmizegetusa Regia – and proceeding towards it while destroying any resistance along the way.

While we have no surviving texts of Trajan's Dacian war, we do have pictures. These spiral up the monument known as Trajan's Column in Rome, as a series of bas-reliefs depicting the war from beginning (the Romans crossing into Dacia) to end (the fall of Sarmizegetusa Regia). The Romans broke down the outer walls of the city, but left the remainder standing once a peace was agreed.

The end

Neither Trajan nor Decebalus regarded the peace as anything more than a stop-gap measure. Hostilities broke out again in dramatic fashion when Decebalus kidnapped a Roman general who was a close friend of Trajan's. Unwilling to be held hostage and used against his emperor, the general killed himself. An outraged Trajan marched on Sarmizegetusa Regia and began a full-scale siege. As was standard practice, the Romans built walls around the city to contain the population (a circumvallation) and cut off the water supply, forcing a surrender.

Decebalus escaped, but was hunted down and killed. Trajan was equally merciless toward his capital. Sarmizegetusa Regia was flattened, apart from that portion where the Romans established a garrison to ensure that the Dacians did not try to rebuild their fortress city. Later, Trajan established a capital for his conquered province some 40 kilometres (25 miles) away, and the last standing walls of Sarmizegetusa Regia were demolished as the army withdrew.

Sarmizegetusa Regia Today

For many years, it was assumed that Sarmizegetusa Regia was identical to Trajan's Roman city of Ulpia Traiana Sarmizegetusa. The latter was rediscovered at the end of the nineteenth century, but the original Sarmizegetusa Regia, being both less accessible and more comprehensively levelled, had to wait a few decades longer.

The true Sarmizegetusa Regia is one of the most dramatic archaeological sites in Romania, with the added bonus that it lies within the spectacular Grădiştea Muncelului Cioclovina Nature Park. Excavation continues, but already enough has been exposed to give modern visitors a good idea of the surprisingly sophisticated life of the inhabitants of this 'barbarian' city.

c. 170 BC–AD 750

Gerasa
A City's Rise and Fall and Rise

One of the most intact cities of the Greco-Roman era outside of Italy itself.

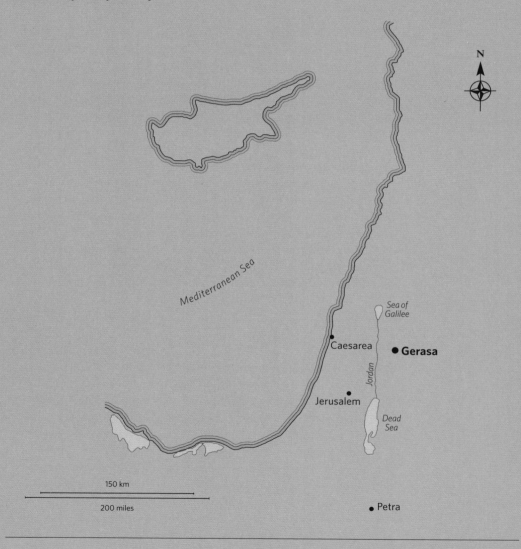

Mediterranean Sea

Sea of Galilee

Caesarea

● **Gerasa**

Jordan

Jerusalem

Dead Sea

150 km

200 miles

● Petra

M odern Jerash (ancient Gerasa) is proof that natural disaster and human-inflicted catastrophes can't keep a good city down. Despite being wrecked by earthquakes and pillaged by invading armies, Gerasa has always recovered. After several centuries of being lost and abandoned, Gerasa has returned to become one of the major cities of the kingdom of Jordan. However, the period of abandonment meant that – unlike many other cities of the period – much of the stonework of the ancient buildings was not recycled into later structures. Ancient Gerasa is one of the most intact cities of the Greco-Roman era outside of Italy itself.

Location, location, location

Gerasa is around 50 kilometres (30 miles) north of the Jordanian capital of Amman, but is a great deal cooler because it sits on one of the highest of the rolling hills that dominate the region.

The south gate of Gerasa was the principal entryway to the city from Amman, the Jordanian capital. This gate was once decorated with carvings and statuary to impress visitors with the city's wealth.

At almost half a kilometre above sea level, the city is relatively free of the oppressive heat of the modern capital and, for several thousand years, has afforded its inhabitants a splendid view over the surrounding countryside.

Today, as in centuries gone by, the hillsides are filled with cedars, alongside orchards of plums, figs and olives. The relatively temperate climate provides good grazing for livestock, and it was probably this factor which convinced the first settlers to make their home there some 7,500 years ago.

Foundation and growth

It is uncertain when Gerasa formally became a city. Some argue that, on the orders of Alexander the Great, the location was chosen by the Macedonian general Perdiccas as a place to settle Macedonian mercenaries after Alexander's successful Egyptian campaign. However, the formal settlement of the city probably happened around 170 BC under one of Alexander's successors, the Seleucid king Antiochus IV Epiphanes.

The settlement was established near an ancient reservoir, with the city's fresh water coming from the Kerwan, a stream

This map with limestone tesserae, excavated from a Byzantine church at Gerasa, shows the Egyptian cities of Alexandria and Memphis.

that flowed through the settlement. The military colonists of the city were quickly joined by merchants who recognized that Gerasa occupied a useful location at the nexus of trade between the port of Joppa (modern Jaffa), Damascus, Petra and the cities of Judaea.

The Judaean connection proved crucial as the Seleucid empire slumped into decay. Unwilling to let a vital trade link fall into hostile hands, the Jewish king Alexander Jannaeus (r. 103–76 BC) besieged and captured Gerasa. The city now acquired a large Jewish population, who seem to have lived relatively peacefully alongside the Macedonians as a part of the Hasmonean kingdom.

The troubles of Roman Gerasa

This was but the first of a series of changes in ownership for the city. When the Roman general Pompey the Great had a serious disagreement with the Hasmoneans, the matter was decisively settled by the Roman legions in 63 BC. Gerasa thus became a Roman city and was later folded into Rome's new province of Syria. As was the Roman custom, Gerasa was left largely to govern itself, which it did as part of a loose confederation of local cities called the Decapolis.

Politics in the Middle East were every bit as turbulent in Roman times as now, as testified by a comment of the Jewish historian Josephus. A massacre of Jews in the coastal town of Caesarea led to retaliation, in which the Jews 'separated into various groups and devastated Syrian villages and the nearby cities of Philadelphia Sebonitis and Gerasa' (*Wars of the Jews* 2.18.1).

Despite – or because of – this, Gerasa was again in Jewish hands at the start of the anti-Roman rebellion that followed immediately afterwards in AD 66. When he retook Gerasa, the Roman general Annius followed the tradition described by the historian Tacitus, whereby the Romans 'create a wasteland and call it peace' (*Agricola* 30).

Gerasa survived this severe depopulation to become a thriving city once more, which came under the jurisdiction of the Roman province of Arabia in AD 106.

Peak Gerasa

This province included the former Nabataean kingdom and the caravan city of Petra. The Nabataean influence can be seen still in the core of Gerasa. Here, on the terraced heights where the temple of Artemis stands, are the ruins of another temple dedicated to the

Previous pages
The Nymphaeum was
the main fountain of
Gerasa. Water was
poured into a stone
basin from fountains
styled as lions' heads.
Such areas were
considered shrines
to water nymphs.

Nabataean god Pakidas. Artemis's temple was the most magnificent, but the city also boasted a splendid temple to Zeus Olympias and others dedicated to Hera, Apollo, Poseidon and Nemesis.

Gerasa now entered a period of unprecedented prosperity. Much of the city had been built on the level ground of a terrace to the left of the Kerwan stream, where city walls almost 3 kilometres (2 miles) long protected the inhabitants. The Cardo Maximus, the main street of the city, ran across this built-up area to the South Gate, but so greatly had Gerasa outgrown its original dimensions that anyone approaching from this direction would pass through 1½ kilometres (a mile) of houses and shops before reaching the city gate.

Near the gate was a hippodrome, where more than fifteen thousand spectators could cram in to watch chariot races. Near the hippodrome stood an arch built to celebrate the visit of the Roman emperor Hadrian to the city in AD 129–30. It says something about the importance of Gerasa that Hadrian's predecessor, the emperor Trajan, also visited – though Trajan's was more of a business trip, during a military campaign in Mesopotamia. Imposing as Hadrian's arch was, Trajan built roads to help with the movement of his armies and, by facilitating trade, these roads were of far greater benefit to the city.

A terracotta figurine
from Gerasa showing
a mix of Greco-Roman
and Oriental style.

A traveller entering the city by the South Gate might proceed directly north along the Cardo Maximus to the city's forum. Given the city's role as a trade centre, this forum was unsurprisingly large – 7,200 square metres (77,500 square feet) – surrounded by imposing columns and paved with limestone slabs. North of that, the road ran uphill to the temple of Zeus, from which the traveller could view the city and the countryside around.

Later Gerasa

During the late imperial period, the Christianization of the empire led to the construction of a large cathedral in Gerasa. Some of the building material was stripped from the temple of Artemis, now deemed surplus to the city's religious requirements. Despite this vandalism the temple still remains one of the city's most imposing structures – and the cathedral bequeathed to posterity some magnificent mosaic floors.

As the Eastern Roman empire became the Byzantine empire, Gerasa remained a centre of some importance – important enough for the Sasanian Persians to raid the place in 614. But while Gerasa seemed able to take all that humanity could throw at it, it was powerless against a massive earthquake that wrecked much of the city in 749. Attempts to rebuild were ruined by further quakes and it seems that for a while the city was abandoned.

Under the Muslim caliphate there was something of a revival. Parts of the city were rebuilt, the local mint started issuing coins, and mosques and churches were in use simultaneously. Sadly, this religious tolerance did not last in the face of religious fanaticism. The Crusaders reached Gerasa in 1121, devastated the city and then promptly abandoned it.

Gerasa Today

Though lost and abandoned for centuries, Gerasa gradually revived, and the new Jerash – built alongside rather than on top of the old one – is a regional capital. The relatively good condition of the Greco-Roman remains attracts tens of thousands of tourists every year. The site itself is somewhat unsignposted, so visitors must rely on the descriptions provided by the expert guides.

There are also two museums, with the older one displaying many artefacts recovered from the ancient city and the more modern Archaeological Museum documenting the storied history of Gerasa over the last seven millennia.

For the last forty years Jerash has also been the venue for an annual festival of culture and the arts, which features artists from across the Arab world and beyond.

Venta Silurum
Life of a Romano-British Town

The most impressive Roman walls surrounding
any town in northern Europe.

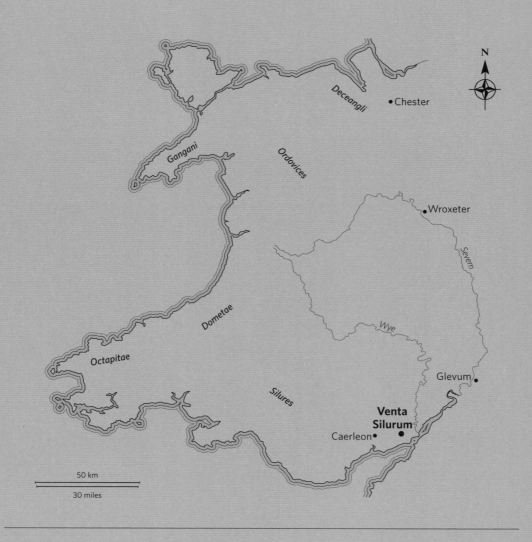

N

Deceangli

• Chester

Gangani

Ordovices

• Wroxeter

Severn

Dometae

Wye

Octapitae

Glevum •

Silures

Venta Silurum

Caerleon • •

50 km

30 miles

A stone head crudely carved from yellow quartz sandstone in Celtic style. Dating from the fourth century AD, this may have represented a household god.

When the Romans invaded Britain in AD 43 they probably did not expect still to be fighting there two decades later. While the southeast fell reasonably quickly (and rose again briefly under Boudicca), the tribes in the highlands of present-day Wales fought the Romans every step of the way. The toughest nut for the Roman legions to crack was a tribe called the Silures, a people whose dark complexions and curly hair caused the historian Tacitus to suppose that their forebears had emigrated from Spain (*Agricola* 11). Ostorius Scapula, the second governor of Britain, proposed in frustration that the Silures should either be extirpated or moved wholesale to a different part of the empire. Scapula died in AD 52, exhausted by non-stop campaigning, and it took another generation before the Silures were forcibly persuaded to accept Roman rule.

A new city

Once they had pacified the Silures, the Romans encouraged the tribe to move into the relatively flat – and much less defensible – lands of what is today the Vale of Glamorgan. There, in AD 75, they set up a small market town to act as the new tribal centre. The name 'Venta Silurum' translates as 'the market of the Silures', with 'Venta' having the same root as the modern word 'vendor'. To make sure that the Silures continued to behave themselves, the Romans established a legionary base a day's march away at Caerleon (Isca Augusta): not so close as to be oppressive, but near enough to quash any thoughts of making trouble. The Silures were considered as *dediticii* – people subject to Roman power who were neither slaves nor citizens.

The town was originally built on either side of the main road between Caerleon and Glevum (Gloucester), where the traffic could suitably impress the locals with Roman military power and economic strength. Since it would defeat the purpose for which the town had been founded, the original site had no defensive walls.

Growing without pains

As the *Pax Romana* took root in Britain, Venta Silurum became an established civic centre, or *civitas*. At the height of empire under the Antonine rulers of the second century, the town began to expand into a tidy little city. There had always been a forum and a basilica, as these were part of the original function of the town (the forum as the marketplace and the basilica for administration and legal matters). Now, as the Silures were given increased control over their own affairs, the basilica was ornamented with Corinthian columns

Though literally dilapidated in places, the walls of Venta Silurum are among the finest examples of Roman-era standing walls anywhere in Europe.

8 metres (26 feet) high, and the *civitas* acquired those very Roman features, an amphitheatre and public baths.

At this point the growing sprawl along the road was regularized and the land was divided into some thirty residential plots, called *insulae*. Many of the houses built on these plots were dual-purpose affairs, consisting of shops or workshops at the front with living quarters to the rear. As time went on, some of the houses became larger and acquired luxury fittings such as mosaic floors and hypocausts (a type of underfloor heating highly desirable in the Welsh climate).

It has been speculated that the legionary base at Caerleon helped the economy of Venta Silurum, not only because the town provided some products to the base, but also because soldiers retired to the city to stay close to the friends with whom they had spent the greater part of their lives. By the late second century the location had become valuable enough, and the Silures peaceable enough, to warrant the construction of an earthen ditch and rampart to defend the town against raiders. More direct military involvement in the town can be seen in a surviving inscription dedicated to the governor Tiberius Claudius Paulinus, which reads 'Paulinus, legate

of Legio II Augusta, proconsul of the province of Narbonensis …
by decree of the *ordines* for public works on the tribal council of the
Silures'. The inscription underlines the close ties between the legion
at Caerleon and the town, and the mention of an *ordo* (tribal council)
shows that the Silures had achieved a good degree of autonomy.

The retreat of empire

This connection was to come to an end in the third century, when the
empire fell into a political and economic crisis. Legio II Augusta was
withdrawn from Caerleon, and this may have prompted the building
of the massive stone walls that surround Venta Silurum to this day.
These walls still stand largely intact, up to 7 metres (23 feet) high in
places. With the increasing threat from Irish pirates raiding up the
River Severn, square towers were built to flank the gates, and there
are signs that the town was defended by a military garrison.

Nevertheless, Venta Silurum suffered from a design fault that
was, literally, built in – the location had been deliberately chosen
because it was hard to defend. Once the Roman legions left Britain,
Venta Silurum was no longer viable. Eventually the townsfolk were
forced to acknowledge this fact and retreat to the greater security
of the nearby hills. Although a monastery was later established on
the site, it seems that for all practical purposes Venta Silurum had
ceased to exist as a civic entity by AD 450.

Venta Silurum Today

Though gone, Venta Silurum continued to loom large in the
consciousness of the local people. The name 'Venta' mutated into
'Guenta' and this eventually became the Welsh kingdom of Gwent.
As Britain became less unruly, a village grew on the site of the former
Roman-era settlement. This was – and is – called Caerwent, with the
'-went' part of the name again derived from 'Venta'.

Because for a long time no-one dared occupy the flat lands upon
which Venta Silurum had stood, the Roman walls were not mined
for stone, as happened in many other places. As a result, the site
retains what are, by some distance, the most impressive Roman
walls surrounding any town in northern Europe.

Most of Venta Silurum is an open-air museum, though a sizeable
portion of the site still remains to be excavated. Visits are possible
all year round and there is a dedicated parking area near the church,
which contains many Roman artefacts from the lost city.

c. 300 BC–AD 256
Dura-Europos
City for Conquest

*Archaeological research has revealed details
of the desperate defence by the Roman garrison.*

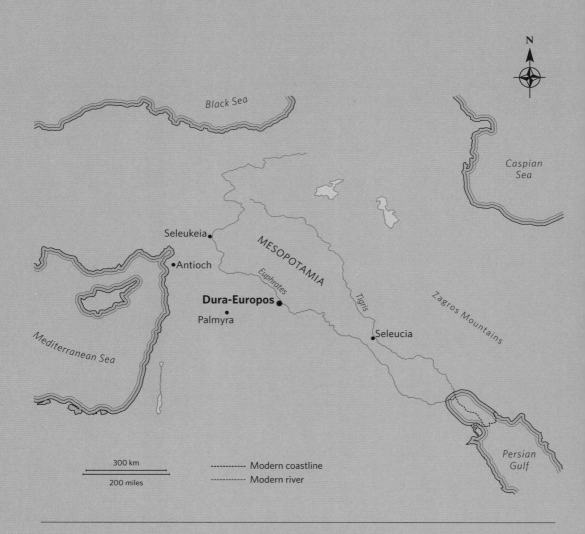

The city known today as Dura-Europos never had more than some fifteen thousand inhabitants. Yet this unremarkable fortress city on the banks of the Euphrates continues to change how we view the ancient world. Within its walls lived a wide cross-section of Mediterranean cultures, representing many religions, including one of the earliest Christian churches yet discovered. The city finally fell after a gruelling siege in late antiquity, which has also revealed the first evidence of the use of poison gas in warfare.

The brooding Roman walls of the lost city form the backdrop to these remains of Dura-Europos, a city that barely gets a mention in ancient texts and is known almost entirely from archaeological research.

Founding

When the city was first founded it was given a functional name to suit its functional purpose. The place was called 'Dura', which can be best translated from the local Aramaic tongue as 'fortress'. The founder was Seleucus I Nicator, a successor to Alexander the Great, who had inherited the Syrian part of the conqueror's domains along with lands stretching eastwards to Bactria in the foothills of the Himalayas.

A wall painting showing the infant Moses found in a *shul* (synagogue) in Dura-Europos. This fortress city was home to a startling number of cultures and belief systems.

Seleucus had recently founded two major cities, which he intended to serve as regional capitals, Antioch and Seleucia-on-the-Tigris. The fortress town of Dura was situated where it could control the Euphrates river crossing on the route between these two, and therefore the expected flow of trade between them. Eventually Dura picked up the alternative name of 'Europos', presumably as a nod to the European origins of Seleucus and the city's garrison of his native Macedonians. However, the hyphenated name of Dura-Europos is modern – it appears that the people living there used either one name or the other.

Development

Thanks to its strategic position as a military base and its location on an inter-city trade route, Dura (Europos) grew into a small but prosperous city, which became the administrative centre for the surrounding territory. In 160 BC the city was damaged by an earthquake and this seems to have prompted the empire's rulers to give their fortress city a do-over to make it the very model of a modern minor urban centre.

The fortress part of town lay to the east, on a narrow ledge well above the river, but below that was a flat area of some 45 hectares (111 acres). This was now given the benefit of sophisticated town planning.

The streets were laid out in rectangular city blocks consistent with the 'hippodamian' model. (Hippodamus developed this town layout for the Greeks in the fifth century BC – ironically by copying it from much older cities in the area around Dura-Europos.) Sewers were dug and the water supply regularized. The city blocks were centred on an agora, which served the inhabitants as a marketplace and public meeting space.

Parthian Dura

While Dura continued to thrive, the same could not be said for the rest of the Seleucid empire. The huge, ramshackle empire was torn apart by centrifugal forces almost from the beginning, and a succession of weak and incompetent rulers did not help. In 113 BC the city fell to the Parthians, an Iranian people who had never greatly liked being ruled by the Greeks.

For the people of Dura the main effect of this change in management was that Seleucia-on-the-Tigris and Antioch were now in different kingdoms, which were not on particularly friendly terms. Therefore, Dura no longer had particular significance either militarily or economically. The town settled down to become just another urban centre in the Parthian empire, notable only for the huge diversity of its inhabitants.

Dura's residents have left us with a fine collection of notes scrawled and scratched on walls in the city, including recipes, names and important dates and even sketches of camel caravans and armoured cavalrymen. These have enabled researchers to determine that the city had a population of Greeks, Arabs, Italians, Jews and Parthians. The elite families that kept a grip on the city's political and economic fortunes seem to have been Greeks from the original Macedonian garrison, who managed to ride out the tides of their city's changing fortunes.

Rome

Astute diplomacy was needed as the growing power of the Roman empire began to threaten Parthian rule. Under the emperor Trajan, Dura briefly became a Roman city in AD 114, but Trajan's successors were unable to hold on to his Mesopotamian conquests and after

Previous pages
The Palmyra Gate of
Dura-Europos shows
that, while some
town gates were
for administrative
purposes or for display,
this city's gates were
designed to keep out
enemies.

a few years Dura became a Parthian possession once again – and the city's elite families held on through it all.

Rome returned for a final time in the AD 160s and the city later became a part of the Roman province of Syria Coele, eventually gaining the prized status of a *colonia*, which gave an advantageous legal status to the inhabitants. The Romans made it clear that this time they were here to stay by turning the northern part of the city into a military base, complete with an amphitheatre to entertain the troops. Legal divorce documents show that some soldiers married local women.

Still, Dura remained an unremarkable city on the imperial frontier. Contemporary histories only fleetingly mention the place, as the writers concentrate on what they consider more important matters. One such was the fall of the Parthian empire and its replacement by the more organized and militaristic Sasanian Persians. This development was to have a huge influence on Dura's future – or rather, its lack of one.

Death of a city

The fall of Dura to the Sasanians is nowhere documented in the historical record, but archaeological research has revealed the details of the desperate defence as the Roman garrison struggled to prevent the enemy from taking the river crossing. Unlike their Parthian predecessors, the Sasanians were experts at siege warfare. Their favourite technique was to dig tunnels under crucial walls and towers and allow the undermined structures to collapse.

The Romans were well aware of the danger and they dug counter-tunnels. The desperate torchlit struggles in the claustrophobic underground tunnels can be seen today from the corpses revealed by later archaeologists. In one tunnel, the Persians realized that the Romans had dug through to them and they retreated, leaving one brave man to ignite a mixture of sulphur and bitumen, which filled the tunnel with poisonous gas. The bodies of nineteen Romans were discovered, along with one Persian. He is assumed to be the man who set off the fumes, but could not make his escape in time.

The heroic struggle by the defenders was in vain – the Parthians eventually tunnelled into the city and destroyed it. While survivors may have lived on for a considerable time amid the rubble, to all intents and purposes, Dura fell in AD 256.

Dura-Europos Today

Before war again convulsed the region in the early twenty-first century, a series of archaeology teams, working with the Syrian government, excavated an astonishing array of documents and artefacts from the ruins. These include the unit documentation for the Roman army's Cohors XX Palmyrenorum, whose archives were found in a good state of preservation, and inscriptions from the first Christian house church ever discovered. Overall, the thousands of artefacts retrieved from the ruins have helped to build a detailed picture of life in the city before its fall.

In recent years Dura-Europos has been looted and largely destroyed by barbarians again. The culprits were members of the so-called Islamic State who, in a desperate attempt to fund their war, ruthlessly pillaged Dura-Europos for relics, destroying an estimated 70 per cent of the site in the process.

800 BC–*c.* AD 650
Beta Samati
Forgotten City of a Forgotten Empire

*The Aksumite empire is one of the largest
empires ever to be forgotten.*

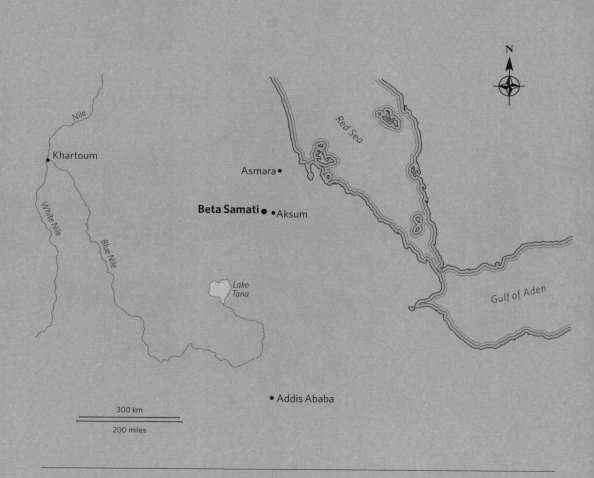

N

Nile

Red Sea

Khartoum

Asmara

Beta Samati • Aksum

White Nile

Blue Nile

Lake
Tana

Gulf of Aden

• Addis Ababa

300 km

200 miles

In the sixth century AD the Persians reckoned there were four great powers in the world: themselves (naturally), the Roman (Byzantine) empire, China and the Aksumites. While most people today are aware of the first three, the Aksumite empire of late antiquity is one of the largest empires ever to be generally forgotten. At its peak in the third century AD the Aksumite kingdom controlled a vast area that included much of modern Ethiopia, Eritrea, northern Sudan and western Yemen.

At this time, caravan routes overland between Europe and Asia had been thrown into chaos by the Age of Migrations, which saw Goths, Vandals, Huns and Slavs moving westward. Since Aksumite power had by then extended to both shores of the Red Sea, the kingdom controlled the most viable trade route between the Byzantine empire and the civilizations to the east. Once the city of Meroë in eastern Sudan fell under Aksumite control, the kingdom also largely controlled what reached the Mediterranean world from sub-Saharan Africa.

Forgotten by the modern world until recently, the role of Beta Samati as an international trading nexus and administrative centre is still being revealed.

Pre-Aksumite era, 775–360 BC

The origins of Beta Samati are still obscure, but radiocarbon dating shows that human occupancy of the site began around 775 BC, two centuries before Rome's traditional foundation date. (Though human occupancy of Rome's Palatine hill had begun thousands of years earlier.) The name of what was then the village of Beta Samati means, in the local Tigrinya language, 'the house of audience' – it may have been where local rulers met petitioners from the surrounding countryside.

At this time Beta Samati would have been under the control of the nearby city of Yeha, 6.5 kilometres (4 miles) away in present-day northern Ethiopia, on the border with Eritrea. Yeha survives as a small town, though with ruins of deep interest to archaeologists. Until recently it was believed that settlement in the area around Yeha largely collapsed after Yeha itself was subordinated by the growing power of Aksum.

Classic Aksumite era, AD 160–380

The Aksumite empire is named after the city of Aksum in the same way that the Roman empire is named after the city of Rome. Aksum is in the central Tigray region of modern Ethiopia, and remains today a town of some sixty thousand inhabitants. The kings who ruled this city and also Beta Samati were cultured individuals, and at least some of them were fluent in Greek. One of the distinctive features of their architecture was the building of giant obelisks that had fake doors and windows carved to make them look rather like modern high-rise buildings.

It is now established that Beta Samati was a thriving economic, religious and administrative centre within the Aksumite kingdom. Relics unearthed at the site show extensive cross-cultural influences. The population dealt with – and may have included – Greeks, Romans, Indians and Arabs. There are suggestions that Greek was the lingua franca, by which the local people communicated with foreign traders. The presence of wine amphorae from the Levant shows that the city not only traded in foreign goods, but also consumed them. Local pottery was somewhat more plain and utilitarian.

Artefacts related to pack animals demonstrate the importance of trade to the city, and workshops indicate that local industry supplied most of the needs of the resident population. The site occupied at least 14.5 hectares (36 acres), and the buildings were densely packed within that space.

This richly worked gold ring with a carnelian stone has an intaglio bull motif, which allowed the ring to be used to seal documents.

A stone pendant with a cross on the left found in the basilica. The language of the writing is Ge'ez, which is still the liturgical language of the Ethiopian Orthodox Church.

Middle to Post Aksumite era, AD 380–900

When King Ezana converted the Aksumite empire to Christianity in the mid-fourth century AD, the population of Beta Samati seems to have had mixed feelings about the new religion. Numerous 'pagan' symbols date from after the town was officially Christianized. The basilica built at this time was a distinctively Christian structure, though it seems to have been used for administration as well as worship.

Beta Samati thrived mainly as a trade hub and as a regional administrative centre. As such, the well-being of the city was dependent on the well-being of the Aksumite empire as a whole. With the rise of the Muslim caliphate of the sixth century, Beta Samati converted to Islam, but this was not enough to save the city. The changing religious and political situation in the region meant that the Aksumite empire no longer controlled the trade corridors upon which its economic health depended.

To add to the kingdom's problems, climate change was desiccating the region, and the productive fields around Beta Samati were changing to the dusty plains that are there today. Some time around AD 960 the Aksumite kingdom quietly collapsed. By then Beta Samati had been abandoned for centuries, with the most recent traces of habitation dating to around AD 650.

Beta Samati Today

Much of what is written about the lost city of Beta Samati is speculative, because the site was rediscovered only in 2009, and the situation in recent years has discouraged further archaeological activity.

The city was found because the Southern Red Sea Archaeological Histories Project began to study the area around Yeha at the turn of the century. Yeha is known to have the oldest standing structures and earliest writing in sub-Saharan Africa, and the researchers were curious as to what else could be discovered.

The local inhabitants directed the researchers to a 'tell', or mound, that rose some 25 metres (82 feet) above the surrounding valley. They knew that this was a place of importance, but all details of its history had been lost. It was quickly established that the tell had been formed by the inhabitants of a city discarding the detritus of daily life in one place for a millennium and a half, creating a city literally built upon the remains of its former self.

The presence of large blocks of dressed sandstone made it clear that this had once been a substantial settlement. In fact, the discovery of Beta Samati has caused a drastic rethink of previous ideas of political and economic activity in the area. Previously it had been considered something of a backwater after the decline of Yeha itself, but it is now clear that trade and commercial activity continued unabated for over a thousand years thereafter. Much of that activity had been transferred to Beta Samati and hidden once the city itself was lost.

As one of the youngest rediscovered cities of the Classical era, Beta Samati remains something of an enigma. A host of questions remain for future researchers to answer once modern political and military issues in the region have been resolved.

Aksumite 'obelisk' probably from the fourth century AD, with a door carved in the base and 'windows' all the way up. These stelae might have served as grave markers, and hundreds of smaller ones have been found in various states of repair.

Before *c.* 750 BC–AD 1923
Derinkuyu
Underground City

Invaders never managed even to discover Derinkuyu, let alone capture it.

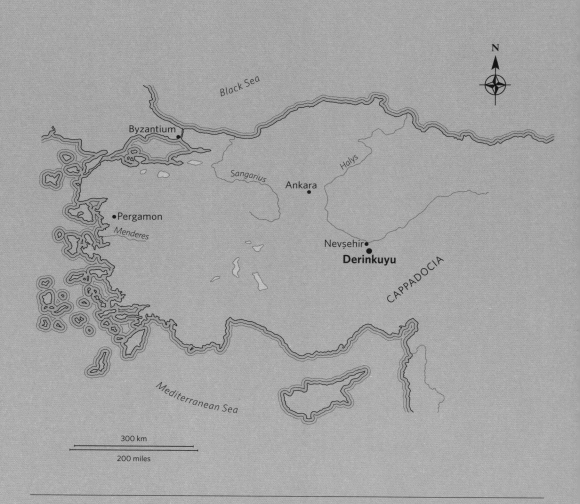

Many people have created a bit more space in their houses by knocking through walls and extending, but only one person has ever managed to expand his living quarters to accommodate some twenty thousand people, along with their goods and livestock. The man in question was living in the Cappadocian province of Nevşehir in Turkey. In 1963 he demolished a wall in his home and discovered a hidden room behind it. This room led to a stairwell, which led to another series of rooms, which led to more rooms, storage areas, tunnels and, as it turned out, to an entire underground city.

Archaeologists have been excavating buried cities for centuries – Pompeii being a prime example. The difference is that this city had not ended up underground through the passage of time or because of a natural catastrophe, but was built that way from the start.

Underground chambers such as this, carved from the tuff, would have allowed the populace to shelter in safety, unknown to invaders on the surface.

Origins

The name of the village where the subterranean city was discovered might have given the locals a clue as to what lay beneath their feet. The site is called Derinkuyu, which translates approximately to 'deep well'. The story of Derinkuyu begins several million years ago when ash from a series of volcanic eruptions covered the landscape. This ash formed a type of deposit called tuff. The fascinating thing about tuff is that it is as easy to excavate as loam, but after being exposed to oxygen, tuff lithifies – which means that it turns as solid as stone. So people can dig through it easily, but end up with a tunnel as firm as if they had dug through bedrock.

It is believed that the first people to take advantage of this at Derinkuyu were the Phrygians, who lived in the area in the eighth century BC. However, there are those who argue that the very earliest chambers were excavated by the Hittites almost a millennium before. What is certain is that the original underground rooms were added to, generation after generation, until the entire secret city was completed in the Byzantine era of the eighth century AD.

There are many other structures, such as cliff houses and even churches, that have been carved out of tuff, and there are even other underground refuges along the lines of Derinkuyu. But no other place in the world is as deep or extensive, or capable of accommodating as many people, goods and livestock.

Fortress city

Another subject of controversy is whether the inhabitants of Derinkuyu were true troglodytes or whether Derinkuyu was an underground fortress, used only in times of crisis. Until the city has been fully explored (and it is so massive that, so far, archaeologists have worked their way through less than half of it) this question will not be fully resolved, though for the present the 'fortress city' hypothesis dominates academic thinking.

Winding tunnels, some with traps, make it unsafe for tourists to wander the underground alone. As some parts of the complex have yet to be fully explored, it might be a long time before a lost visitor is discovered.

There can be no question that Derinkuyu was built with defence in mind. The city doors would do credit to a modern nuclear bunker. They are made of solid stone, half a metre (2 feet) thick, in the shape of giant wheels. They were rolled into place into a slot across the entrance, effectively making that entrance as solid as the walls alongside. Were attackers able to batter through these doors, they would have to proceed at a crouch, in single file, through narrow, low-ceilinged corridors.

They would eventually emerge one by one into a higher-roofed room, where a well-armed reception committee would be standing upright to meet them. (Several rooms have been located that might have served as armouries.) Even if attackers managed to navigate the (deliberately?) confusing maze of tunnels – some of which had dead ends – and capture a level, the defenders could retreat to a similarly fortified lower level and do it all over again.

In all, depending how one counts, Derinkuyu has sixteen or eighteen levels extending to a depth of 70 metres (230 feet) underground. There are no indications that invaders ever managed to discover Derinkuyu, let alone capture it.

Home sweet cavern

The advantage of taking several thousand years to construct an underground refuge is that there is plenty of time to correct mistakes and add amenities. When people were not using Derinkuyu as their primary residence, the caverns were apparently used for storage. With the lower parts deep underground, the temperature is a constant 13–15° Celsius (55–59° Fahrenheit) all year around. A carefully designed ventilation system of fifty-two major air shafts and numerous minor vents keeps the air fresh at even the deepest levels.

Some wells in the city reach to the surface, but as an attacker might poison these, the inhabitants also dug wells that were accessible only within the underground city, along with other vertical shafts to take care of sewage. Conditions were excellent for the long-term storage of grain, and there were several underground bakeries to make sure that the inhabitants had a regular supply of fresh bread. Other underground rooms served as stables for livestock, and doubtless some storage rooms contained large bales of hay. Olive and wine presses stored in the caverns show that at least some of the harvest might have been kept safely underground for processing.

It has been speculated that one particularly large underground space served as a school or meeting place, with small rooms set into the main hall that might have been offices or studies. The numerous inscriptions in Greek found on the walls indicate that for centuries the city served as a place of refuge for Christians. The changing religious climate in Anatolia meant that Christian communities were under threat from persecution first during the Roman imperial era, and again in the centuries of warfare between the Muslims and the fading Byzantine empire. When the Ottomans took over Turkey, Derinkuyu was again a place of refuge, and yet again during the massively destructive invasion of the Mongols under Timur (Tamerlane) in the fourteenth century.

Forgotten Derinkuyu

It is uncertain when Derinkuyu slipped out of memory. One of the key elements of a secret city is that people do not publicize or record it. We know that the Greek peoples of the area called the place Malakopea, and its current name of Derinkuyu came into regular use in the 1910s and 1920s when the Cappadocian Greeks used the tunnels to escape periods of persecution. In the early twentieth century, the last users quietly sealed the entrances and departed for the safer environs of Greece, without telling the new occupants of the site what lay beneath.

Thereafter, the hidden city of Derinkuyu slumbered undisturbed until one of the secret entrances fell into the hands of an ambitious home improver.

Derinkuyu Today

Since 1969, parts of Derinkuyu have been open to the public. Trips underground are strictly supervised, since there is a real danger that any straying tourist might not be seen again for a long time.

Tourist trips are often arranged from Göreme, a town some 30 kilometres (18½ miles) away, allowing travellers to enjoy the excellent scenery along the route. Being completely weatherproof, the caverns are open all year round, though the opening times differ in summer and winter.

Very recently another set of hidden tunnels has been found beneath a castle in the same province. Some excited archaeologists reckon that this hidden city, revealed by work on a housing project, may be even larger than Derinkuyu.

EPILOGUE

Everyone walking through a ruined city has tried to imagine the place in its prime – the bustling thoroughfares, the exotic temples, the crowded marketplaces. Yet how many have looked at the streets of their home town and tried to imagine how they might appear to archaeologists, two thousand years hence? That shopping centre, with the walls collapsed and newly excavated basements open to the sky, fragments of pavement meticulously brushed clean and plastic plates carefully extracted from rubbish piles and taken away. Perhaps some future archaeologist will stand in the debris of a teenager's bedroom and pronounce that, on the basis of the artefacts within, it was either a brothel or a shrine.

For the first time in millennia, there is actually a question of whether cities are necessary, and whether they can – or should – survive. People once gathered together to share resources and knowledge and to collectively experience civil and religious events. Yet today, with extended manufacturing and distribution systems, it is possible for even those dwelling in remote towns to shop for a wider range of goods than were available in London or New York even a few decades ago. It is no longer necessary to live in the same city, or indeed on the same continent, as one's employer, and millions now view sporting and state events over broadcast media of better and better quality. Academic research that could once be tackled only in a university town can now be done on a mountainside by a hermit with the right equipment. In short, are we now cresting a wave of urbanism, where most of humanity is crammed into cities that technology is already making obsolete?

It is hard to believe this when looking at the neon-lit centre of Tokyo, or the morning rush hour in Los Angeles. Yet the same sense of permanence and wonder at the scale of human endeavour must have gripped the inhabitants of Çatalhöyük as they gazed at the walls of humankind's first city. Deep inside, we know that the cityscapes we see around us are ephemeral, and that whatever our great-grandchildren experience, it will not be the city of today. Today's cities are cramped, polluted, expensive and – as we have recently discovered – superb incubators of disease. Yet they also offer, as cities have always done, a way of life unmatched in richness and excitement.

With a changing climate, we can be sure that places like Pavlopetri will not be the last cities to vanish beneath the sea nor, like Timgad, be abandoned to the desert. A more enduring question is whether in a few centuries' time there will be any cities at all on Earth, other than relics preserved so that academics and tourists can marvel at a human experiment in communal living that lasted for over six thousand years.

Further Reading

PART ONE **The Oldest Cities**

Çatalhöyük

Balter, M., *The Goddess and the Bull: Catalhoyuk: An Archaeological Journey to the Dawn of Civilization* (New York, 2010).

Hodder, I., 'Women and Men at Çatalhöyük', *Scientific American* 290(1) (2004), pp. 76–83.

Hodder, I., *Çatalhöyük Excavations. The 2009–2017 Seasons* (Ankara, 2023).

Skara Brae

Clarke, D. V., *Skara Brae: Official Souvenir Guide* (Edinburgh, 2012).

Shepherd, A. N. et al., 'Skara Brae Life Studies: Overlaying the Embedded Images', in F. Hunter and A. Sheridan (eds), *Ancient Lives: Object, People and Place in Early Scotland. Essays for David V. Clarke on his 70th birthday* (Leiden, 2016), pp. 213–32.

Watterson, A. et al., 'Digital Dwelling at Skara Brae', in I. Russell and A. Cochrane (eds), *Art and Archaeology: Collaborations, Conversations, Criticisms* (London, 2014), pp. 179–95.

Akkad

Black, J. A., *The Literature of Ancient Sumer* (Oxford, 2006).

Foster, B. R., *The Age of Agade: Inventing Empire in Ancient Mesopotamia* (Abingdon, 2015).

King, L., *A History of Sumer and Akkad* (London, 1994).

Liverani, M., 'Akkad: The First World Empire: Structure, Ideology, Traditions', *History of the Ancient Near East/Studies* 5 (1993), pp. 1–10.

Speiser, E. A., 'Some Factors in the Collapse of Akkad', *Journal of the American Oriental Society* 72(3) (1952), pp. 97–101.

Pavlopetri

Harding, A., 'Pavlopetri: A Mycenaean Town Underwater', *Archaeology* 23(3) (1970), pp. 242–50.

Holden, C., 'Undersea Metropolis', *Science* 324 (2009), p. 995.

Ivrou, V., *The Maritime Cultural Landscape in the South Peloponnese-Kythera-West Crete During the Late Bronze Age*, PhD thesis, University of Glasgow (2014).

Zoar

Dishi, G., 'Saving Zoar: How Did Lot Succeed?', *Jewish Bible Quarterly* 38(4) (2010), pp. 211–18.

Donner, H., *The Mosaic Map of Madaba: An Introductory Guide* (Leuven, 1992).

Neev, D. and Emery, K., *The Destruction of Sodom, Gomorrah, and Jericho: Geological, Climatological, and Archaeological Background* (Oxford, 1995).

Hattusa

Beckman, G., 'Hattusa', in R. S. Bagnall et al. (eds), *The Encyclopedia of Ancient History* (Hoboken, NJ, 2013).

Bryce, T., 'The Last Days of Hattusa: The Mysterious Collapse of the Hittite Empire', *Archaeology Odyssey* 8 (2005), pp. 32–41.

Charles River Editors, *Hattusa: The History and Legacy of the Ancient Hittites* (2016).

Mardaman

Barjamovic, G. et al., 'Trade, Merchants, and the Lost Cities of the Bronze Age', *The Quarterly Journal of Economics* 134(3) (2019), pp. 1455–1503.

Millard, A. R., 'History and Legend in Early Babylonia', in V. P. Long et al. (eds), *Windows into Old Testament History: Evidence, Argument, and the Crisis of "Biblical Israel"* (Grand Rapids, MI, 2002), pp. 103–10.

Plantholt, I. S., 'Gula in the 2nd and 1st Millennia BCE', *The Image of Divine Healers: Healing Goddesses and the Legitimization of the Asû in the Mesopotamian Medical Marketplace* (Leiden, 2017), pp. 51–105.

Thebes

Pischikova, E. et al., *Thebes in the First Millennium BC* (Newcastle, 2014).

Strudwick, N. and Strudwick, H., *Thebes in Egypt:*

A Guide to the Tombs and Temples of Ancient Luxor (Ithaca, NY, 1999).
Warburton, D., *Architecture, Power, and Religion: Hatshepsut, Amun & Karnak in Context* vol. 7 (Münster, 2012).

Phaistos
Charles River Editors, *The Phaistos Disc: The History of the Indecipherable Ancient Minoan Artifact Found on Crete* (2018).
Schoep, I. et al., *Back to the Beginning: Reassessing Social and Political Complexity on Crete during the Early and Middle Bronze Age* (Oxford, 2011).
Vasilakis, A., *Agia Triada Phaistos* (Heraklion, 2009).

PART TWO **From Troy to Rome**

Troy
Hertel, D., 'The Myth of History: The Case of Troy', *A Companion to Greek Mythology* (Oxford, 2011), pp. 425–41.
Rose, C., *The Archaeology of Greek and Roman Troy* (Cambridge, 2013).
Winkler, M. M., *Troy: From Homer's Iliad to Hollywood Epic* (Hoboken, NJ, 2009).

Thonis
Belov, A., *Ship 17: A Baris from Thonis Heracleion* (Oxford, 2019).
Robinson, D. and Goddio F., *Thonis-Heracleion in Context* (Oxford, 2015).
Shenker, J., 'How Thonis-Heracleion resurfaced after 1,000 years under water', *The Guardian* (15 August 2016).

Mycenae
Chadwick, J., *The Mycenaean World* (Cambridge, 1977).
French, E. B., *Mycenae, Agamemnon's Capital: The Site and its Setting* (Stroud, 2002).
French, E. B. et al., 'Archaeological Atlas of Mycenae', *Archaeological Society of Athens Library* 229 (2003).
McCabe, R. and Cacouri, A., *Mycenae: From Myth to History* (New York, 2016).

Seleucia-on-the-Tigris
Hopkins, C., *The Topography and Architecture of Seleucia on the Tigris* (Ann Arbor, MI, 1972).
Messina, V., 'Seleucia on the Tigris. The New Babylon of Seleucid Mesopotamia', in R. Matthews and J. Curtis (eds), *Mega-cities & Mega-sites. The Archaeology of Consumption & Disposal. Landscape, Transport & Communication* vol. 1 (Wiesbaden, 2012).
Oetjen, R., *New Perspectives in Seleucid History, Archaeology and Numismatics: Studies in Honor of Getzel M. Cohen* vol. 355 (Berlin, 2019).

Sybaris
Kleibrink, M., 'The Search for Sybaris', *BABesch* 76 (2005), pp. 33–70.
Lomas, H., 'Sybaris', *Oxford Research Encyclopedia of Classics* (Oxford, 2016).
Rutter, N., 'Sybaris–Legend and Reality', *Greece & Rome* 17(2) (1970), pp. 168–76.

Plataea
Boedeker, D., 'Heroic Historiography: Simonides and Herodotus on Plataea', *Arethusa* 29(2) (1996), pp. 223–42.
Buckler, J. and Spawforth, A., 'Plataea', *Oxford Research Encyclopedia of Classics* (2016).
Rissman, E., *Plataea* (Madison, WI, 1902).

Taxila
Ahmed, N., *The History and Archaeology of Taxila*, PhD thesis, University of London, School of Oriental and African Studies (1958).
Marshall, J., *Taxila 3 Volume Paperback Set: An Illustrated Account of Archaeological Excavations* (Cambridge, 2013).
Shah, S., 'Legendary History of Taxila', *Ancient Sindh Annual Research Journal* 10(1) (2008), pp. 97–131.

Tigranocerta
Coloru, O., 'Tigranocerta', in R. S. Bagnall et al. (eds), *The Encyclopedia of Ancient History* (Hoboken, NJ, 2013).
Orr, C., *Tigranes the Great: A Re-Appraisal*, BA thesis, University of Wales Trinity Saint David (2016).
Sinclair, T., 'The Site of Tigranocerta (II)', *Revue des Études Arméniennes* 26 (1996), pp. 51–117.

Persepolis

Barnett, R., 'Persepolis', *Iraq* 19(1) (1957), pp. 55–77.

Mousavi, A., *Persepolis: Discovery and Afterlife of a World Wonder* (Berlin, 2012).

Razmjou, S., 'Persepolis: A Reinterpretation of Palaces and their Function', in J. Curtis and S. J. Simpson (eds), *The World of Achaemenid Persia* (London and New York, 2010), pp. 231–45.

Numantia

Cheesman, G., 'Numantia', *The Journal of Roman Studies* 1 (1911), pp. 180–86.

Goffaux, B., 'Numantia (Spain)', in R. S. Bagnall et al. (eds), *The Encyclopedia of Ancient History* (Hoboken, NJ, 2012).

PART THREE **Across the Roman Empire**

Glanum

Congès, A., 'Glanum', in R. S. Bagnall et al. (eds), *The Encyclopedia of Ancient History* (Hoboken, NJ, 2012).

Heyn, M., 'Monumental Development in Glanum: Evidence for the Early Impact of Rome in Gallia Narbonensis', *Journal of Mediterranean Archaeology* 19(2) (2006), pp. 171–98.

Kleiner, F. S., *The Glanum Cenotaph: A Study of the Great Relief Panels* (New York, 1973).

Falerii Novi

Battistin, F., 'Space Syntax and Buried Cities: The Case of the Roman Town of Falerii Novi (Italy)', *Journal of Archaeological Science: Reports* 35 (2021).

McCall, W. F., *Falerii Novi and the Romanisation of Italy During the Mid-Republic*, PhD thesis, The University of North Carolina at Chapel Hill (2007).

Verdonck, L. et al., 'Ground-penetrating Radar Survey at Falerii Novi: A New Approach to the Study of Roman Cities', *Antiquity* 94(375) (2020), pp. 705–23.

Cyrene

Abdulkariem, A. and Bennett, P., 'Libyan Heritage Under Threat: The Case of Cyrene', *Libyan Studies* 45 (2014), pp. 155–61.

Jeffery, L., 'The Pact of the First Settlers at Cyrene', *Historia: Zeitschrift für Alte Geschichte*, 10(2) (1961), pp. 139–47.

Reynolds, J., 'Cyrene', *Oxford Research Encyclopedia of Classics* (Oxford, 2015).

Tipasa

Briggs, L. C., *Archaeological Investigations Near Tipasa, Algeria. With Geological Comments by Charles E. Stearns*, ed. H. Hencken (Cambridge, MA, 1963).

Ford, C., 'The Inheritance of Empire and the Ruins of Rome in French Colonial Algeria', *Past & Present* 226 (2015), pp. 57–77.

Nadir, M., *The Revaluation of the Archaeological Sites of Tipasa: Contribution to the Safeguard of the Algerian Heritage* (2022).

Baiae

Capozzi, R. et al., 'Archaeology, Architecture and City: The Enhancement Project of the Archaeological Park of the Baths of Baiae', *ArchNet-IJAR: International Journal of Architectural Research* 10(1) (2016), pp. 113–30.

Painter, K. S., 'Roman flasks with scenes of Baiae and Puteoli', *Journal of Glass Studies* 17 (1975), pp. 54–67.

Petriaggi, B. D. et al., 'Reconstructing a Submerged Villa Maritima: The Case of the Villa dei Pisoni in Baiae', *Heritage* 3(4) (2020), pp. 1199–1209.

Volubilis

Benton, J., 'The Bakeries of Volubilis: Process, Space, and Interconnectivity', *Mouseion,* 17(2) (2021), pp. 241–72.

Picard, C. and Grummel, W., 'Volubilis: French Excavations at a Moroccan City' *Archaeology* 2(2) (1949), pp. 58–65.

Skurdenis, J., 'Passport: Road to Volubilis', *Archaeology* 41(3) (1988), pp. 50–55.

Stabiae

Maiuri, A., *Pompeii, Herculaneum and Stabiae* (Milan, 1963).

Orsi, L., 'The Excavations at Stabiae', *East and West* 4(2) (1953), pp. 101–108.

Purcell, N., 'Stabiae', *Oxford Research Encyclopedia of Classics* (Oxford, 2016).

Maiden Castle

Redfern, R., 'A Re-Appraisal of the Evidence for Violence in the Late Iron Age Human Remains from Maiden Castle Hillfort, Dorset, England', *Proceedings of the Prehistoric Society* 77 (2013), pp. 111–38.

Russell, M., 'Mythmakers of Maiden Castle: Breaking the Siege Mentality of an Iron Age Hillfort', *Oxford Journal of Archaeology* 38(3) (2019), pp. 325–42.

Sharples, N. M., *English Heritage Book of Maiden Castle* (London, 1991).

Timgad

Cherry, D., *Frontier and Society in Roman North Africa* (Oxford, 1998).

Kherrour, L. et al., 'Archaeological Sites and Tourism: Protection and Valorization, Case of Timgad (Batna) Algeria', *Geo Journal of Tourism and Geosites* 28(1) (2020), pp. 289–302.

Antinopolis

Abdulfattah, I., *Theft, Plunder, and Loot: An Examination of the Rich Diversity of Material Reuse in the Complex of Qalāwūn in Cairo* (2017).

Lambert, R., *Beloved and God: The Story of Hadrian and Antinous* (London, 1984).

Vout, C., 'Antinous, Archaeology and History', *The Journal of Roman Studies* 95 (2005), pp. 80–96.

PART FOUR The Empire's Edge and Beyond

Palmyra

Denker, A., 'Rebuilding Palmyra Virtually: Recreation of its Former Glory in Digital Space', *Virtual Archaeology Review* 8(17) (2017), pp. 20–30.

Sommer, M. and Sommer-Theohari, D., *Palmyra: A History* (Abingdon, 2017).

Veyne, P., *Palmyra: An Irreplaceable Treasure* (Chicago, 2017).

Waldgirmes

Rasbach, G., 'Germany East of the Rhine, 12 BC– AD 16. The First Step to Becoming a Roman Province', in R. G. Curcă et al. (eds), *Rome and Barbaricum: Contributions to the Archaeology and History of Interaction in European Protohistory* (Oxford, 2020), pp. 22–38.

Schnurbein, S. von, 'Augustus in Germania and his New "Town" at Waldgirmes East of the Rhine', *Journal of Roman Archaeology* 16 (2003), pp. 93–107.

Wells, P., *The Battle That Stopped Rome: Emperor Augustus, Arminius, and the Slaughter of the Legions in the Teutoburg Forest* (New York, 2004).

Sarmizegetusa Regia

Comes, R. et al., 'Enhancing Accessibility to Cultural Heritage Through Digital Content and Virtual Reality: A Case Study of the Sarmizegetusa Regia UNESCO Site', *Journal of Ancient History and Archaeology* 7(3) (2020), pp. 124–39.

Florea, G., 'Sarmizegetusa Regia – the Identity of a Royal Site?', in C. N. Popa and S. Stoddart, *Fingerprinting the Iron Age – Approaches to Identity in the European Iron Age. Integrating South-Eastern Europe into the Debate* (Oxford and Philadelphia, 2014), pp. 63–75.

Oltean, I. and Hanson, W., 'Conquest Strategy and Political Discourse: New Evidence for the Conquest of Dacia from LiDAR analysis at Sarmizegetusa Regia', *Journal of Roman Archaeology* 30 (2017), pp. 429–46.

Gerasa

Haddad, N. and Akasheh, T., 'Documentation of Archaeological Sites and Monuments: Ancient Theatres in Jerash', *Conservation of Cultural Heritage in the Arab Region* 61 (2005), pp. 64–72.

Holdridge, G. et al., 'City and Wadi: Exploring the Environs of Jerash', *Antiquity* 91(358) (2017), pp. 1–7.

Khouri, R., *Jerash: A Frontier City of the Roman East* (Hoboken, NJ, 1986).

Venta Silurum

Howell, R., *Searching for the Silures: An Iron Age Tribe in South-East Wales* (Cheltenham, 2009).

Frere, S. and Millett, M., 'Venta Silurum', *Oxford Research Encyclopedia of Classics* (Oxford, 2016).

Guest, P., 'The Forum-Basilica at Caerwent (Venta Silurum): A History of the Roman Silures', *Britannia* 53 (2022), pp. 1–41.

Wacher, J., *The Towns of Roman Britain* (Abingdon, 1997).

Dura-Europos

Baird, J. A., 'Dura-Europos', in T. Kaizer (ed.), *A Companion to the Hellenistic and Roman Near East* (New York, 2021), pp. 295–304.

Baird, J. A., *The Inner Lives of Ancient Houses: An Archaeology of Dura-Europos* (Oxford, 2014).

Brody, L. and Hoffman, G., *Dura-Europos: Crossroads of Antiquity* (Chicago, 2011).

Beta Samati

Burstein, S. M., *Ancient African Civilizations: Kush and Axum* (Princeton, NJ, 2009).

Cartwright, M. and Davey, A., 'Kingdom of Axum', *Ancient History Encyclopedia,* retrieved from https://www.worldhistory.org/Kingdom_of_Axum/ (last accessed 7 February 2023).

Harrower, M. et al., 'Beta Samati: Discovery and Excavation of an Aksumite Town', *Antiquity* 93(372) (2019), pp. 1534–52.

Derinkuyu

Çiner, A. and Aydar, E., 'A Fascinating Gift from Volcanoes: The Fairy Chimneys and Underground Cities of Cappadocia', in A. Çiner, C. Kuzucuoğlu and N. Kazancı (eds), *Landscapes and Landforms of Turkey* (Edinburgh, 2019), pp. 535–49.

Mutlu, M., *Geology and Joint Analysis of the Derinkuyu and Kaymaklı Underground Cities of Cappadocia, Turkey*, MA thesis, Middle East Technical University, Ankara (2008).

Pinkowski, J., 'Subterranean Retreat May Have Sheltered Thousands of People in Times of Trouble', *National Geographic* (26 March 2015).

Sources of Illustrations

2–3 Photo Michael Runkel/imageBROKER/Superstock; 4 Yale University Art Gallery, New Haven. Yale-French Excavations at Dura-Europos; 6–7 Photo Ali Balikci/Anadolu Agency via Getty Images; 8 Photo DeAgostini Picture Library/Scala, Florence; 11 Cleveland Museum of Art. Leonard C. Hanna, Jr Fund 1964.359; 12 Photo DeAgostini/W. Buss/Getty Images; 17 Çatalhöyük Research Project; 18 Photo Sonia Halliday Photo Library/Alamy Stock Photo; 21 Çatalhöyük Research Project. Photos Jason Quinlan; 23 Photo VisitScotland/Colin Keldie; 24–25 Stromness Museum. Photo Rebecca Marr; 26–27 Photo David Lyons/age fotostock/Superstock; 29 National Museums of Scotland. Photo © National Museums Scotland; 31 The Metropolitan Museum of Art, New York. Gift of Nanette B. Kelekian, in memory of Charles Dikran and Beatrice Kelekian, 1999; 32 Musée du Louvre, Paris; 35 Ashmolean Museum, University of Oxford. Presented by Herbert Weld-Blundell, 1923. Photo Ashmolean Museum/Bridgeman Images; 37 Photo N. Maverick/Adobe Stock; 38 Photo © BBC Archive; 41 Photo panosk18/Adobe Stock; 43 Photo Manuel Cohen/Scala, Florence; 44 Hessisches Landesmuseum Darmstadt; 46–47 Photo Jane Taylor/Shutterstock; 49 Photo Zev Radovan/Alamy Stock Photo; 51 The Metropolitan Museum of Art. Purchase, Joseph Pulitzer Bequest, 1955; 52–53 Photo Sailingstone Travel/Adobe Stock; 54 Cleveland Museum of Art. Leonard C. Hanna, Jr Fund; 55 Photo funkyfood London – Paul Williams/Alamy Stock Photo; 57 Bassetki-Project of the University of Tübingen. Photo Peter Pfälzner; 59 Private collection; 60 Bassetki-Project of the University of Tübingen. Photos Rouhollah Zarifian; 63 Photo Tomasz Czajkowski/Adobe Stock; 64 Los Angeles County Museum of Art. Gift of Carl W. Thomas; 66–67 Photo Andrew McConnell/robertharding; 68 Los Angeles County Museum of Art. Purchased with funds provided by Phil Berg; 71 Photo Gianni Dagli Orti/Shutterstock; 72 Photo DeAgostini/Superstock; 75 Heraklion Archaeological Museum; 76 Photo Christoph Gerigk © Franck Goddio/Hilti Foundation; 81 Photo Archive Photos/Stringer/Getty Images; 82–83 The Walters Art Museum, Baltimore. Acquired by Henry Walters with the Massarenti Collection, 1902; 85 Antikenmuseum Basel und Sammlung Ludwig; 86 Städel Museum, Frankfurt am Main; 89, 91 Photos Christoph Gerigk © Franck Goddio/Hilti Foundation; 95 National Archaeological Museum, Athens; 96 National Archaeological Museum, Athens. Photo Leemage/Corbis/Getty Images; 98–99 Photo aerial-photos. com/Alamy Stock Photo; 100 J. Paul Getty Museum, Los Angeles; 101 The Metropolitan Museum of Art. Rogers Fund, 1954; 103 Musée du Louvre, Paris. Photo VCG Wilson/Corbis/Getty Images; 104 Yale University Art Gallery, New Haven; 105 New York Public Library. Photo Science History Images/Alamy Stock Photo; 106 Photo Yphoto/Alamy Stock Photo; 109 Photo Alfonso Di Vincenzo/KONTROLAB/LightRocket via Getty Images; 110 Yale University Art Gallery, New Haven. The Ernest Collection in memory of Israel Myers; 111 Museo Nazionale Archeologico della Sibaritide. Photo by DeAgostini/A. De Gregorio/Getty Images; 112–13 Photo DeAgostini/Superstock; 115 Bibliothèque nationale de France, Paris. Photo Artokoloro/Alamy Stock Photo; 116 Schloss Bruchsal. Photo INTERFOTO/Alamy Stock Photo; 119 The Metropolitan Museum of Art, New York. Rogers Fund, 1906; 121 Photo grandpa_nekoandcoro/Adobe Stock; 122 clockwise from left: The Metropolitan Museum of Art. Rogers Fund, 1913; Cleveland Museum of Art. Gift of George P. Bickford 1956.1; Los Angeles County Museum of Art. Purchased with funds provided by the South and Southeast Asian Acquisition Fund and the Southern Asian Art Council; Cleveland Museum of Art. John L. Severance Fund 1982.66; 124–25 Photo Ms Mariko Sawada, Saiyu Travel Japan; 126 Los Angeles County Museum of Art; 127 The Metropolitan Museum of Art. Samuel Eilenberg Collection, Gift of Samuel Eilenberg, 1987; 129 Photo courtesy of Hamlet Petrosyan; 130 Private collection; 132 J. Paul Getty Museum, Los Angeles. Ms. Ludwig XIII 5, v2 (83.MP.148.2), fol. 82v. Digital image courtesy of the Getty's Open Content program; 135 Photo Borna Mirahmadian/Adobe Stock; 136 The Metropolitan Museum of Art. Fletcher Fund, 1939; 137 Photo Andre Chipurenko; 138–39 Photo Kurt and Rosalia Scholz/Superstock; 141 Private collection; 143 Photo Prisma Archivo/

Alamy Stock Photo; **144** Photo Tolo/Adobe Stock; **146** Junta de Castilla y León. Archivo Museo Numantino. Photo Alejandro Plaza; **147** Museo del Prado, Madrid; **148** Photo Michael Runkel/robertharding; **153** Photo Carole Raddato; **154–55** Photo Dominique Reperant/Gamma-Rapho/Getty Images; **156** Photo Paul Popper/Popperfoto via Getty Images; **158** Hôtel de Sade, Saint-Rémy-de-Provence. Photo Gianni Dagli Orti/Shutterstock; **161** Photo Scala, Florence; **163** Musée du Louvre, Paris. Photo Musée du Louvre, Dist. RMN-Grand Palais/Thierry Ollivier; **164, 165** The Metropolitan Museum of Art. Purchase by subscription, 1896; **167** The British Museum, London; **168–69** Photo Atlantide Phototravel/Getty Images; **171** The British Museum, London; **173** Photo DeAgostini/C. Sappa/Getty Images; **174** Photo Werner Forman/Universal Images Group/Getty Images; **176–77** Photo lic0001/Adobe Stock; **179** Musée archéologique de Tipasa. Photo Jona Lendering; **181** Photo Beniamino Forestiere/Shutterstock; **182** Fitzwilliam Museum, Cambridge; **185** Photo BIOSPHOTO/Alamy Stock Photo; **187** Photo Gianni Dagli Orti/De Agostini/Getty Images; **188–89** Musée Archéologique, Rabat. Photo DeAgostini/Superstock; **190** Photo Petr Svarc/imageBROKER/Shutterstock; **193** National Archaeological Museum, Naples. Photo Scala, Florence; **194, 199** Photo Adriano/Adobe Stock; **196–97** Photo Rocco Casadei/EyeEm/Adobe Stock; **198** The Minneapolis Institute of Art; **201** Dorset Museum; **202–203** Photo Skyscan Photolibrary/Alamy Stock Photo; **207** Photo World Photo Service LTD/Superstock; **208** Timgad Archaeological Museum. Photo mauritius images GmbH/Alamy Stock Photo; **210** Photo Michel Huet/Gamma-Rapho/Getty Images; **213** Art Institute of Chicago; **215** Musée du Louvre, Paris; **216** clockwise from top left: Harvard Art Museums/Arthur M. Sackler Museum. Gift of Dr Denman W. Ross. Photo President and Fellows of Harvard College; The Metropolitan Museum of Art. Rogers Fund, 1909; Musée du Louvre, Paris. Photo funkyfood London – Paul Williams/Alamy Stock Photo; **218** Photo Karol Kozlowski/age fotostock/Superstock; **223** Los Angeles County Museum of Art. Gift of Robert Blaugrund; **224** Photo Christophe Charon/Abaca Press/Alamy Stock Photo; **227** Cleveland Museum of Art. Purchase from the J. H. Wade Fund 1970.15; **228** Los Angeles County Museum of Art. Gift of Nasli M. Heeramaneck; **231, 232, 235** Deutsches Archäologisches Institut; **234** Kunstmuseen Krefeld; **237** Museum of Dacian and Roman Civilisation, Deva. Photo DeAgostini/Superstock; **238** Photo robertharding/Alamy Stock Photo; **240** Photo Coroiu Octavian/Alamy Stock Photo; **243** Photo Targa/age fotostock/Superstock; **244, 248** Yale University Art Gallery, New Haven. The Yale-British School Excavations at Gerasa; **246–47** Photo Andrea Jemolo/Scala, Florence; **251** Newport Museum and Art Gallery; **252** Photo DeAgostini/G. Wright/Getty Images; **255** Photo DeAgostini/Getty Images; **256** The Jewish Museum, New York. Photo Godong/UIG/Shutterstock; **258–59** Photo Jane Taylor/Shutterstock; **261** (left) Yale University Art Gallery, New Haven. Yale-French Excavations at Dura-Europos; **261** (right) The Metropolitan Museum of Art. Rogers Fund, 1916; **263, 264, 265** Courtesy Michael J. Harrower. Photos Ioana A. Dumitru; **266** Photo Artushfoto/Adobe Stock; **269** Photo Kadir Kara/Alamy Stock Photo; **271** Photo Jackson Groves/The Journey Era; **274** Photo DeAgostini/Superstock

Index

Dedicated to Ludwik Dziurdzik

Part opener captions:

Intro
p.8 Nike (Victory) stands at the prow of
a trireme in a third-century BC monument
celebrating a naval victory by the people
of Cyrene (in modern Libya).

Part One
p.12 The great temple of Amun in Karnak,
Egypt. The view here is of the first of
ten 'Pylons' or gateways leading to the
complex, which is one of Egypt's great
archaeological treasures.

Part Two
p.76 Colossal statue of Hapy, ancient
Egyptian god of the Nile, strapped with
webbing before being cautiously raised
out of the water of Aboukir Bay, Egypt.

Part Three
p.148 Trajan's Arch at Timgad, Algeria.
Standing 12 metres (40 feet) tall, the arch
commemorates the emperor's founding
of the city. It was embellished later with
further sculptures, including one of the
goddess Concordia presented by the later
emperor Septimius Severus.

Part Four
p.218 The Roman South Theatre Stage
in Gerasa, Jordan. Theatre was one vehicle
by which Greco-Roman culture was spread
across Rome's multi-ethnic empire.

Epilogue
p.274 Statues of Demeter and Kore stand
amid the ruins of their temple in Cyrene, Libya.

First published in the United Kingdom in 2023
by Thames & Hudson Ltd, 181A High Holborn,
London WC1V 7QX

First published in the United States of America in 2023
by Thames & Hudson Inc., 500 Fifth Avenue, New York,
New York 10110

Lost Cities of the Ancient World © 2023
Thames & Hudson Ltd, London
Text © 2023 Philip Matyszak
Maps by Martin Lubikowski

British Library Cataloguing-in-Publication Data
A catalogue record for this book is available from
the British Library

Library of Congress Control Number 2023937744

ISBN 978-0-500-02565-9

Printed in China by RR Donnelley

FSC
www.fsc.org

MIX
Paper | Supporting
responsible forestry
FSC® C144853

Be the first to know about our new releases,
exclusive content and author events by visiting
thamesandhudson.com
thamesandhudsonusa.com
thamesandhudson.com.au